I0040225

ASK
POWER
QUESTIONS

A Practical Guide
to Help You Get What You Want
in Business, Life, and Friendship

By
SANDY NELSON

Ask Power Questions
A Practical Guide to Help You Get What You Want in
Business, Life, and Friendship
By Sandy Nelson

Published by Meet Your Muse Press
Copyright 2015 Sandy Nelson. All rights reserved.

All rights reserved. No part of this book may be reproduced in any form or by any electronic or mechanical means including storage information or retrieval systems—except in the case of brief quotations embodied in critical articles or reviews—without permission from its publisher, Meet Your Muse Press, 4921 5th Avenue South, Minneapolis, MN 55419.

Although every precaution has been taken to verify the accuracy of the information contained herein, the author and publisher assume no responsibility for any errors or omissions. No liability is assumed for damages that may result from the use of information contained within.

Books may be purchased by contacting the publisher and author at: sandy@meetyourmuse.com
Edited by Barbara Millman Cole
Cover Design by Spilled Ink Studio

Nelson, Sandy 1954-
Ask Power Questions:
A Practical Guide to Help You Get What You Want in
Business, Life, and Friendship

Library of Congress Control Number: 2015919008
ISBN 13: 978-0692573815
ISBN10: 069257381X

1) Types of questions 2) Interview questions 3) Creativity Coaching techniques 4) Appendix of powerful questions

First Edition Printed in the United States

Praise for Ask Power Questions

"Sandy Nelson has done a remarkable thing in her new book *Ask Power Questions*. Not only does she clearly explain what power questions are and why you want to employ them in your daily life, she presents you with actual power questions that you can use in all sorts of settings, from chatting with your cab driver to dealing with your boss to providing care for a parent. Not to mention dealing with your lawyer and your hair stylist! This is highly useful book that you really shouldn't miss!"

—Eric Maisel,
Life Purpose Boot Camp and *The Future of Mental Health*

"Ask Power Questions is a valuable resource that gives instructions for inspiring and effective communications. This practical and intelligent guide can benefit anyone and everyone. Keep it handy and use it often!"

—Beverly R. Down, President & CEO,
Creativity Coaching Association

"Ask Power Questions is about much more than questions, but about questing, language, and meaningful communication. It is written with humor, anecdotes and wisdom, and explores useful questions for everything from creative moments to business environments to emergencies. We can all learn a lot from this work."

—Karl Schlotterbeck, MA, CAS,
psychologist and author

"Author Sandy Nelson brings to life the *'art of asking power questions.'* Through her brilliant storytelling and with a creative perspective, she guides the reader to look closer at life's situations by asking questions that inspire a deeper meaning, a more innovative approach - and that yield to a heightened sense of self-discovery and self-empowerment. Sandy's own experience as an artist provides the perfect backdrop for many of her teaching stories. This is a book that I'll be referring to when I find myself stuck on how to move forward in an authentic and meaningful way - and one that I'll be recommending to all my clients."

—Tina M. Games,
certified creativity and life purpose coach,
and author of *Journaling by the Moonlight:
A Mother's Path to Self Discovery*

Acknowledgements

Writing a book is an enormous journey through one's own mind. It took a small village to help me accomplish capturing my ideas, and choosing my thoughts. I am thankful to my husband and partner of forty years, Jeff Nelson, who is capable of supporting me and my art, bold enough to utter his insights and honest criticism, and can still love me in the midst of creative chaos. I give many thanks for the blessings of my two sons, Ben and Alex Nelson, both of whom offered inspiration, creativity, a bit of playfulness, and countless opportunities for me to learn and practice the material in this manuscript. Thank you to my mentor, Eric Maisel, who kept my creative fires stirred and me focused to reclaim this project many times over and see it through to completion. I especially wish to thank my editor and writing coach, Barbara Millman Cole, for her ability to bring out my best wordsmith proclivity, her patience, and her edits, which skillfully nestled my thoughts between the covers. And I give special thanks to the many friends, associates, and clients who graciously shared their questions and experiences.

Author Note

The information within these pages is equally useful for men and women. Throughout this book I use the pronoun "she" for ease of reading.

Table of Contents

Chapter One

Questions and Strategies - The Challenge of Rumpelstiltskin

"To be able to ask a question clearly is two-thirds of the way to getting it answered."

- John Ruskin

What is a power question? A power question is one that directly yields the desired answer(s). These are not the answers you may think you want; rather, they are the ones you need.

To perform effectively and provide an environment in which to grow in your world, you need to formulate questions. Not just any questions, but the most powerful questions you can create. To question powerfully, you need to know the purpose of your quests. Powerful questions set a strong focus in motion, and with this focus you will manifest a moving wave of creation directed at receiving your request.

In the tale of Rumpelstiltskin, a trial is presented to a young woman who is said to spin straw into gold. Of course she can't. So, to save her life, she pays an elf who can spin the gold for her. Tragically, she promises her first born child to the elf in exchange for more spun gold — that is, unless she can guess his name. The woman, now queen and fully aware of her purpose, uses strategy to formulate the focused questions necessary to learn the elf's name, saving her child.

Many versions of how this story unfolds exist, all ending with the riddle answered. While Rumpelstiltskin's question held the power of life and death over the Queen, the question itself was rather simple, "What is my name?" Power questions don't need to be complex and often are subtle or simplistic. They just need to create the context in which the best information can be exchanged between the one who is questioning and the one who has the answer.

Rumpelstiltskin asked a simple power question. That question created a situation requiring the queen to formulate her own concerted power question in order to the meet the challenge and resolve the problem. "In the time allotted me, how do I discover this magician's true name and thereby save my child?"

Just as fairies, and the characters they encounter, unwind riddles in their tales, in real life we are all faced with challenges that appear as questions to solve. Some are worth the effort, but many are not. As you master the skills set forth in this book, you'll discover you can decide what challenges you'll accept and how to recast them in the formula you need for your own success. You're not Rumpelstiltskin, and your goal is not to create a guessing game of magical questions and answers; rather, you will learn specific techniques to help you get right to the point so you can first discover and then ask the best power questions for your creative quest.

Power Questions Go Beyond What We Want to What We Need

Sometimes, power questions can be surprisingly simple. What time do we need to leave to arrive on time? What time will you be ready for me to pick you up? Power questions can also be creative and multifaceted. What type of gear will be most useful on a long mountainous hike in the desert? Either way, the goal of the power question is to help you focus and get what you're after.

Questions get us what we want. Powerful questions go beyond what we want to get us what we need. We use different styles of questions to learn and find our way. We define our individuality and build relationships by asking ourselves introspective questions. Our wealth depends on posing great financial questions. Our health can only thrive through probing lifestyle questions. How do we develop pertinent questions to yield pertinent answers?

In our own minds, massive bits of information churn in fragments. When we question, we begin to formulate thought. Productive action can only follow thought. Focused questioning helps us to organize thought so it is useful. So, power questions are a necessary part of our mental functioning. Without them, we often fall victim to chaotic thought. And, sadly, our lives follow.

> "A spell perhaps?" The prince wrinkled his face as if it physically hurt him to think and ask questions." - Liz DeJesus

I like fairytales because they have happy endings — however, to get what you want in life, you can't live in a fairytale. And, you certainly can't speak in riddles or rhymes if you want people to understand your life quest. You will need to figure out your own answers to life, and to do so, you'll need to formulate your own great questions.

Asking a question is simple. Getting the correct answer is not.

Two friends meet:
> "What's that frown about?"
> "I had another awful day. I hate my boss!"
> "Uh oh, what did he (or she) do now?"

A client and coach meet.
> "What's that frown about?"

"I had another awful day. I hate my boss!"

"What are you willing to do for yourself, in order to change this situation?"

We've all felt it, the zinger when the conversation turns. That's the "POW!" That's the often uncomfortable meaning within the powerful question asked. That's the question that demands attention by waking you up and directing you to act. If you want to get what you want in life, you have to ask powerfully.

We think. We ask questions. We have lots of thoughts whirling in our heads most of the time. While we may understand what we're thinking, other people may not. Being clear enough in our own thoughts to figure out there is something we need does not mean we're necessarily able to clarify our needs to someone else.

We often resist the changes that challenge us. This is a fight that cannot be won. As the quaint saying goes, we have to "go with the flow".

Questions help you navigate the flow of change. And, since this change is constant, asking power questions becomes the strong vessel you'll need to get you where you want to go. Great minds have contemplated theories around getting great results; thus, to get a great answer, you have to ask a great question.

When you master your questions, you master your life. You won't be masterful by asking just any questions. You need to ask the power questions. In one way this sounds very simple, but in another, it is pretty hard for many people to focus upon and figure out. Have you ever felt stumped answering this question: What do you really want?

"What do I truly want?" is a robust question that deserves a fully ripe answer, and one that only you can honestly ask and answer. That's why it can be a tough question. When I coach people, this is often the pivotal question that redirects their lives. In some poetic circles, the question is considered the answer, and when you master asking power questions, this concept will become clearer.

Creativity Coaches Cut Through the Mental Chatter to Nurture Your Creative Soul

I wrote "Ask Power Questions" because as a professional creativity and life purpose coach, I want to help creative people define and realize their quests. Many people don't truly understand what I can do for them because mine is a relatively new field of professional service. Basically, I listen to a client's description of her situation and help to formulate the questions she is trying to ask. Usually, clients are dealing with a challenge and need some help to figure it out. Most of us can solve our problems with careful self-analysis; however, it isn't easy to hear ourselves through all of the mental chatter. That's where a good coach can help. I listen for the clues and collect them; then, I give them back in my voice so my clients can hear their own thoughts. I help keep track of preset goals and keep the process moving forward. I simplify, clarify, affirm, and provide the platform for my clients to manifest their own successes.

As a coach, creativity workshop developer/ facilitator, and fine artist, I have developed expertise in the area of creativity. I understand the elements of the creative process, as well as the types of people who need to create. This includes the sometimes devilish reasons why certain kinds of folks *must* create. True meaning and derived purpose can be both exhilarating and exhausting, requiring much from the creative individual. As an artist myself, I can draw from both professional and personal experience to understand the creative process and help other artists come to their own self-understanding.

From time to time, we all benefit from having a little help to do the things we must or to accomplish new things we yearn to try. Along our way, we can get discouraged, dismantled, depressed, and plain stuck. Often, working with a coach provides clues to help highlight the creative individual's need for care. Creating art takes more than wishful thinking or just plain magic to manifest meaning out of thin air. Artists need to be supported and nurtured. My brand of creativity coaching includes care for the creative soul, because if the soul of an artist droops, her passion may lag, and without her zest, it's pretty hard to create. This downward cycle can lead to all sorts of nasty outcomes.

While I have an assortment of skills I use to provide my service, my main tool is the power question. It is the power question that opens each journey, and it is the sum of the power questions posed that defines the traveled path. It is the power question that becomes the primary focus of creative work. So it is my quest, as coach, to introduce you, as creative soul, to your power questions.

I See the Trail of Asking Great Questions

I perform many activities in my own life that require me to figure out the order of my approach; I write, coach people, and make art. One particular area of art I enjoy is painting.

When I paint, I navigate my canvas with questions. What's the tone of this picture? What shapes will dominate? Where do I need more repetition? Shall I use Rose Madder or Viridian to mix my shadows?

To make a painting is to go on a quest. To create a great painting, I must go on a great mission of risky exploration and profound discovery. I have to infuse my mission with deep passion. If I want to claim value in what I seek, I need to make it the best quest I can.

When I look at my paintings, I can see the trail of questions that led me through the process of laying paint here and scraping it off there. The movement of color exposing mistakes reveal my moments of discovery. Trends emerge. Many paintings ripen into muddiness, reflecting my mucking around, as I try new ideas and test my limits.

In my studio I have a pile of rejected paintings. They have issues with color, design, or other aspects relating to artistic merit. They also reveal the trend of fuzzy focus on my part. Without clearly thinking through what I want to achieve with my painterly efforts, I risk missing the clarity and, thus, the meaning I want to impart through my work. If my quest is mediocre, insincere, and lacking clear direction, I'm not using powerful questions.

The process of painting, like living to one's fullest potential, requires many things; but, for the purpose of this illustration, consider talent and skill. Talent relates to my distinctive, instinctive abilities on numerous levels and helps define what I want to do. Skill is what I develop in myself so I can do what I want to do. My talent determines what I want to paint. My skill determines my ability to paint what I want.

Without asking deep questions about what I want my painting to express, I'm haphazardly going through the motions of painting and only relying on my talent to reach for success. It's like rolling the dice and hoping to get lucky. To consistently make good paintings, I need both talent and skill.

In the world of painting, there are technical skillsets to master, such as the chemical properties of the paint, the way the paper or canvas is made, or the type of brush or palette knife and the mark it makes. Then there are the various ways one can use these tools to create art. With practice, an artist can develop her skill using the tools of her trade.

One of the most important artistic skills is thought. This is the critical mass of any great art. Every aspect of painting presents the artist with multiple questions. Deciding which questions are the most poignant to tell the story of what the art is about is the key skill of every great artist.

When I have a good painting, I see the trail of asking great questions. How will the size of this piece imply a relationship with the viewer? From which viewpoint will I reveal this imagery? Am I telling a story or asking a question on this canvas? Which specific techniques will I use to portray the emotional tone, and what direction will I choose to lead the viewer through? My painting has become powerful because I asked power questions.

I've learned the level of success achieved in life directly relates to the quality of the questions asked during the challenge of realizing that success. The greatest of my achievements have come from asking power questions.

Navigating the Modern Communication Maze and My Book

I wanted to write a commonsensical, simple, easy-to-read, but more importantly, useful book about how to ask a good question. There are plenty of authoritative books about the proper use of words and language; however, we don't actually talk that way. We just don't speak proper English the way it is written. So why ask your questions that way?

Language, like the force of nature, is always changing. It is the product of human communication. So, as we evolve, our words and questions must adapt. New words enter into modern vocabulary and older words may phase out. But more importantly, how we use language as a tool matters, and that is what is changing most. My book is about how to utilize language to cut through the chatter and express your focused thoughts; how to formulate your most clear questions in order to gather the best information you need to fulfill your creative quests.

The recent advent of cell phones and tablets have dramatically altered the way we quest. We're more likely to check things out online before we engage actual people. This can be helpful. We can often answer our own questions by looking things up on any number of Internet service sites, and we can learn a lot about the way a multitude of people around the globe are talking.

Unfortunately, the downside to our technical world is that it can be perilous to real-time human connection. It drives me crazy when I'm speaking to a live customer service representative who tells me to "just go on the website." If I didn't want to contact a real person, I would have done that, but I did make the effort to connect live and in person, so why am I being redirected to an impersonal machine? Folks are also distracted by their tech tools and often only halfway focus on what you may be asking. This leads to endless sidetracks and repetitive work to find the answers you seek.

I think you'll find many of my 17 Strategies will help you navigate through this modern communication maze. To communicate well, you will need to adjust your approach and ask power questions.

I organized this book in two parts. The first half explains what a power question is and how to quest powerfully; the benefits of asking power questions; and my methods, which include 17 Strategies to help you succeed in your own powerful quests.

In the Appendix, the second half of my book, I created actual sample questions for you to use. Some questions are subtle, while others are bold. Beginning with dialogue openers useful for questioning anyone, an alphabetized list follows that illustrates how you might question the types of people you connect with daily, as you move along your journey in and out of differing micro-cultures. Use them, as written or merely as inspiration, to personalize questions for yourself as you embark on your own great and powerful quests.

If you manage other people or are a creative person engaged in living an artistic life, all of the questions on the list may come in handy at one time or another, but feel free to use them in ways they're most helpful to you.

Great creative people use both parts of their brain in harmony. They can think critically and creatively, and they are effective at getting what they want, because they know when to use the left or right side of their brain. As if tuning a kaleidoscope, their critical and creative thoughts are able to merge and organize when they consciously focus. If you're in an industry where you need to master handling many differing viewpoints and facts, all at the same time, remember it's easy to let these opinions and facts slip over into your communications. However, this can lead to misunderstandings if these tidbits of information are given out willy-nilly, without forethought. As you read on, you'll discover the tools you will need to remain clear and focused, as well as enable you to help those you engage do the same.

Chapter One Summary Power Questions

What do you hope to gain from reading this book?

What powerful quest do you want to take?

What is the most difficult question anyone asked you?

What is the hardest communication style you've encountered?

How have you used questioning to further your own life quests?

Chapter Two

The 17 Strategies —
Why Did the Ant Survive
while the Grasshopper Perished?

"Strategy is about making choices, trade-offs; it's about deliberately choosing to be different."

- Michael Porter

My life has been full of amazing experiences and bizarrely unusual circumstances. In order to survive them, I had to ask key questions. However, to thrive, I learned to *ask power questions*. I wrote this book to help others find a useful way to navigate their own quests for success.

I sure appreciated the help I got along my way. So I've devised 17 Strategies to help you master asking great and powerful questions. Seventeen strategies may sound like a lot, but how many of the hundreds of fairytales can you name? In comparison, it only takes a few simple tricks to undo the magical thinking we conjure in our own impish reality. These Strategies are my tricks. Sharing them is my way of passing along the gifts I received when I needed them most. I know that in order to get what you want, you're going to have to ask power questions. My "17 Strategies to Formulate Power Questions" will show you how.

Asking a question is negotiating for the information you want. How many times have you been asked to get to the point? Have you ever asked yourself just what the point is? Sometimes, it's hard to find the right context to frame what you want. In any good negotiation, there has to be a win-win resolution. By quickly getting to the powerful part of your quest, you are making the win-win a reality for the other person, too.

In the fairytale "The Ant and The Grasshopper", the ant anticipated the upcoming event of winter, and made a plan to prepare for what she needed. She had a good strategy and survived the winter with enough food for herself and her fellow ants, while the grasshopper suffered and, in many versions of the story, died. The moral is that it is best to prepare for times of necessity. The ant made a strategy to make sure she gathered the plentiful bounty of summer to ensure the best outcome of the barren winter when food would be hard to come by. And her fellow ants helped her. But the grasshopper, only thinking of the present and content to laze away the hours enjoying summer, never even thought to question what he would do come winter.

> "If I had an hour to solve a problem and my life depended on the solution, I would spend the first 55 minutes determining the proper question to ask, for once I know the proper question, I could solve the problem in less than five minutes." - Albert Einstein

Years ago, I was in a car accident and suffered head injury that damaged the language center of my brain. I spent a year in a concussive fog, unable to clearly communicate what I was feeling. I was incapable of asking clear questions. Frustrated, I persevered and continued with my treatments to relearn the skillsets needed to fully converse. One idea that struck me was to not ask just any questions, but to ask the most powerful questions I could. Questions are plentiful, but well-formed questions must be constructed with careful thought. To construct a great sentence, I needed to find strategies for myself.

I didn't want to settle for learning to communicate minimally. I wanted to communicate better than I had before my accident. Like the ant, I had to make a plan to gather what I needed, to not only survive, but thrive. I've gathered what I learned into a list of 17 Strategies that have helped me, and now have helped many of my clients develop the skill to formulate and ask their own power questions.

In order for you to ask the most powerful questions you can, you'll probably need to refer back to these 17 Strategies until you've mastered them. You'll use some in all quests and others for special circumstances. Together, they will help you navigate the art of asking power questions. I'll discuss how you can use them in more detail in the following chapters. Some chapters are devoted entirely to one Strategy while others help you learn the sense of using several Strategies combined.

17 Strategies to Formulate Power Questions

1. Know what you want.

Ever chat with an inquisitive soul who rapid fires questions at you? You can't answer the first one before they ask another, and another. You get confused because they are. They don't bother to figure out what they want to know. And as a result, your conversation is not only chaotic, but meaningless. Face it, many of us tend to do this when we haven't thought through what we want to know. So take the time you need, and figure out what you want from the conversation before you start asking questions.

Do you want to know the time? What kind of time? The time it is right now, as marked on a watch by hours and minutes? Or the time it actually takes to get somewhere? What about the time it will take to drive to a certain building in rush hour? And then by what route? Knowing what you want helps you to be very clear about what information you need to know.

2. Know what you're willing to negotiate.

Being aware of what you're willing to negotiate is important for your quest. Everything in life is based on give and take. Cause and effect can work to your advantage if you bother to make it your ally. Ever ask a question of a stranger, only to have the person answer with, "What's in it for me?" That's an honest answer, because most of us are thinking it, even if we don't say it out loud. Be upfront with what you're willing to give to get your information.

People have to take time away from their own thoughts to answer yours. Play fair. Here are a few examples: "I see you're busy, but if you could answer my question, I can get out of your way much quicker." Or, "Will you have the time by this afternoon to gather the information I need so I can get back to you by tomorrow with my final report?"

3. Listen carefully and without letting your emotions interfere.

This can be a hard tactic to manage. However, it is essential to get what you want. If someone or circumstance has you emotionally charged up, letting loose of your self-control won't help. Yelling, crying, or acting out will only clutter up the communication and cause you a delay to get your request answered.

Listening and being compassionate will usually do the trick. Just observe what the other person is saying. Pretend you are a recording device and just gather the words. If you really must get an answer, and you are just unable to control your emotions, use a recorder (smart phones are great for this) and listen to the answer after you regain your senses. This is a good practice anyway, especially if there are many details you need to capture. Learn much more about the magic of listening in Chapter Five.

4. Be calm and open. Breathe.

No one likes it when someone rushes them or cuts them off. It doesn't matter whether you're in a line, traffic, or conversation. If you want to be powerful, you need to be peaceful in your approach when you ask your questions. Breathing is a gift in this instance. Watch your own breath, and make it slow and rhythmic. Did you know it's true that you can actually calm someone else down by slowing down your own breath? Use this skill to your advantage. If you can ask your question in a lower voice, you're calm.

5. Hold your own character and characterizations back.

You may have a great personality, but if you pepper your requests with your charm, you may confuse your audience and never get what you want. Resist putting your persona out front, and just ask in simple terms.

Watch out for your own characterizations. They may be true for you, but they are a bias. We all have them, and some can be downright nasty to someone else's way of being. Racism, bigotry, sexism are all forms of our own classifications. Our brains work this way, but some of what we actually believe might make it hard for us to play outside our own play lot. If you find you have asked someone a question they find offensive, apologize! Then, if you can, try to ask your question again without offending. Simply keep to the actual facts of what you need.

6. Be clear and concise.

One of my favorite bits of conversational learning my husband and I have had the pleasure of gaining through our relationship is this:

- Be blunt
- Be brief

- Be gone

It works like a charm! How many times have you had to listen to someone else ramble on explaining why they're asking you for something? Or maybe you hear yourself do it and notice the pained impatience on your listener's face. Just ask your question, hear the answer, and move on. If you're a female talking to a male, this may be an essential skill for you to master. Men really don't take in a large amount of word information. It's just the way they're wired. If you're a male asking a female for something, be careful not to sound dictatorial or demanding. Women tend to react negatively when they hear an authoritarian tone from a man.

7. Don't confuse.

Don't repeat your questions with new words. This is a nasty habit we all seem to have. Understand that when you restate your question with new or different words, your listener hears another question. As I mentioned, I experienced some language and hearing damage from an auto accident. For a while, I had to ask people what they said over and over because, either I couldn't actually hear them, or I couldn't comprehend what the words meant. Every time, rather than repeat the exact words, people would rephrase what they said, which only flooded my mind with too much new information. Lots of folks have hearing loss, and others have a short attention span, so asking your questions using too many variations will become confusing. Remember to repeat the words you actually spoke at least three times before you try to reframe your question.

8. Stay focused on your quest.

Don't get distracted or let others sidetrack your quest. It's human nature to embellish what we hear. Make sure you keep your focus directed at the outcome you seek. Otherwise, you'll end up in a dialogue that leads you to someplace you didn't intend to go. Asking a question is a form of conversation, but it really isn't a dialogue full of interesting back and forth comments. Questioning is a straightforward process of using words to gain specific information, and nothing more.

9. Be patient.

Ah, Patience! This is truly a virtue in our current, hurry-up lifestyle. Give people a few moments to slow their speed, both in their physical existence and within their own mind, and then they can focus on you and what you're asking of them.

10. Recognize differences.

Variety is the spice of life, so let it be in your quests, too. Different cultures, even within relatively close proximity, have major differences in the way they share information. Watch for these unfamiliar communications. They can be entertaining, and you can learn something new, as well as get your answers.

11. Navigate and be a navigator.

Remember, this is *your* quest. Be in charge of it by navigating through the obstacles and passages that are part of the process. Don't expect other people to figure out the way you need to find your information. Instead, lead them through the maze. Show them the way you want to go. Don't ask, "How do I find the restrooms by the subway?" Do say, "I'm walking to the redline subway on Broad Street. Can you direct me to the restrooms there?" When you navigate in this way, you tell people how you want to receive your information, and it's much easier for them to answer.

12. Get responses, not reactions.

Getting informative responses instead of confused reactions can be a tricky skill to learn, and I've devoted an entire chapter (Chapter Seven) to this strategy. If you get a reaction from people when you ask your question, but not the information you need, you may need to reflect on what you're saying, or the way you say it. You could be asking in a way that is offensive, or your question may not actually make any sense. Check your words and see if they need a rephrase.

Sometimes, it is the person you ask, too. So choose the people who would probably know the answer and not just someone you feel more comfortable talking to. Imagine you're in a strange city and need directions. There are three people standing on the street in front of you. One is your sex and similar in age, milling about; another is younger and the opposite sex, hailing a cab; and the third is a policeman. Who would be best for you to ask?

13. Know the types of questions.

Most people don't realize there are numerous kinds of questions. Each type is designed for a purpose. To be an effective questioner, you'll need to know the types, and when and how to use them.

There are questions formed to get a yes/no answer and a slight variation to receive a direct response. If you want to learn something about how a person feels, you'd use a sensory, dreaming, or perhaps a fill-in-the-blank form. A coach regularly uses pointed, exploratory, goal-setting, and exit questions. I share plenty of examples and more detail about where power questions come from and the many types of questions in Chapter's Six and Seven.

14. Be creative and playful.

A quest is an adventure, so have some fun with it. You'll also wake up other people, intrigue them with your quest or spark ideas for their own quests, when you are creative or play with the process of asking them your questions. I don't mean "play" in ways that annoy, or belabor the point of getting what you want, but in ways that make the quest interesting to engage the other person. In Chapter Eight we'll explore many options for using your creativity and playfulness to enhance your power quests.

15. Use the right voice.

How you use your voice is an important tactic that is often misunderstood and overlooked. If you're a woman, asking in a high-pitched, squeaky voice or using baby talk is just plain painful to hear. Stop yourself and speak as low as you can with adult language. If you're a man, don't use a loud voice because it's scary to listen to. Also, for both sexes, don't be angry or vulgar. And I do need to say you should speak directly to your audience and not through your ongoing phone conversation - it's very disrespectful. Chapter Nine will help you learn great ways to speak your questions.

16. Beware of Dialogue Snatchers.

We all have to deal with these disruptors. If you use most of the other Strategies, you'll be able to manage the majority of these types of dialogue-stealing people. However, there are a few special techniques you can employ for the tough ones; for instance, gently talking down an agitated person, using focus tricks for those with personality or mental afflictions, and learning to establish clear cut boundaries with controlling types. This is a big Strategy to comprehend, and I'll explain much more in Chapter Ten.

17. Use HALOS.

I've found this to be an easy way to remember the key points of asking powerful questions. This simple acronym stands for:
    Hear

Articulate

Listen

Observe

Sift

"HALOS" can be used as a quick checklist. Am I actually hearing? In other words, am I actually comprehending what the words spoken to me mean? Am I articulating clearly so my message makes sense? Am I listening to what is being spoken back to me? Am I observing the interaction or interfering in the answer? Am I sifting through the information to make sure this is the answer I want?

Pointers to Help Before You Start Your Quest

Using these 17 Strategies will help you gain the answers you seek. Each chapter will delve deeper into a particular Strategy or combine Strategies for you to learn the technique of creating your own power quest.

Before you start your quest, keep a few pointers in mind. Generally, it's really important to know a bit about what you want to know and also about the person you're asking. Take a moment to figure out what you want before you ask your questions.

Remember, we all have focus challenges in our expanding global world that present us with new territory to explore. If you're asking for directions from someone who has ADD, you'll need to keep your question simple and repeat it *exactly*, and as often as necessary, to help them focus on what you want to know. It's pretty easy to spot this condition in a conversation because the answer you get will most often quickly race all over the place, flooding your communication with extra information. Just keep your question simple and direct, and be patient as your listener centers on what you need to know. Might you have a similar communication challenge with someone whose language you don't speak fluently? Imagine all the possible individuals you will encounter who will test your communication skills in your quest.

Think your power question through, and trust your gut: Why are you asking *this* person? *What* are you asking *of* this person? Don't rely on someone else's brain to solve your problems if you can figure it out for yourself. Know what you want to get from your question and be clear about it. If you don't know what you want and are not clear about it, your line of questioning can become annoying, because you're really exercising another agenda called "fix it for me." Be respectful toward the people you question, and show them you are also respectful by the way you ask your questions.

To be a power questioner, you have to be a great listener. I'm surprised at how many people find it odd that when they ask a question, they need to listen carefully. Being a good listener is the other important half of good communication. I wrote an entire chapter on the topic of listening. Remember, in order to truly hear what another person is saying, you'll need to:

- Open your ears
- Open your mind
- Close your mouth

Pay close attention to all the cues you get from the people you are asking your question. Watch their body language (and your own). Are they focusing on or distracted with their own activity? Do they truly know the answer to your question? Do they want to help you? It never hurts your quest to simply first ask, "Can you help me?"

You might be surprised to learn just how many people need to be reminded to stop talking and listen. Ah-hem, all of us, at one time or another, need this reminder. If you're not getting the answers you want — maybe you're not listening.

At the end of each chapter, I'll mention which of the 17 Strategies I discussed and offer some food-for-thought questions to help you assimilate my ideas about asking powerful questions.

In addition to identifying the 17 Strategies that will help you power quest, this chapter introduced Strategies:

1. Know what you want.

2. Know what you're willing to negotiate.

3. Listen carefully and without letting your emotions interfere.

Chapter Two Summary Power Questions

In which circumstances do you communicate at your best?

Are you most comfortable speaking in a group or individual setting?

What do you like about engaging social networks?

What are your most useful technical tools?

Which of the 17 Strategies seem most likely to be of help to you?

Chapter Three

Know What You Want -
What was Goldilocks Thinking?

"Very few beings really seek knowledge in this world. Mortal or immortal, few really ask. On the contrary, they try to wring from the unknown the answers they have already shaped in their own minds - justifications, confirmations, forms of consolation without which they can't go on. To really ask is to open the door to the whirlwind. The answer may annihilate the question and the questioner."

- Anne Rice

"Who's been sleeping in my bed?" "Who's been eating my porridge?" "Who's been sitting in my chair?" The three bears were wise enough to know what to ask to find out who was messing with their stuff. That's great for them. However, this tale is a simple, vague kind of quest, and I never have figured out what Goldilocks was trying to find.

Food, rest, sleep, are all what she availed herself of, but perhaps she didn't know she wanted these things before she stumbled upon the house in the woods. A main point of the story is that she took all without asking or thinking of any consequences. Though she just happened upon the house and decided to go in, she did not think her actions through, nor ask herself what she was really after.

The principle behind any good quest is to know what you want to get. It's assumed you know, because you're asking.

We explore through our questions. We may consider a solution or a reaction, but we quest our way to these results. That's why I like coaching other people so much. Questioning is a natural part of communication, and we question most of the time. However, we don't all do it well. Many of us don't know how to ask questions, and many don't know how to listen to the answers.

When I'm coaching, I ask the tough and important questions. You know, they're likely the ones you'd rather not think about; however, they're the very questions that get you what you want.

The act of asking a powerful question is usually not that difficult, though I offer a few tips. However, figuring out a powerful question can be a challenge. No matter who you are, developing the sensibilities that create the skills needed to analyze, sequence, and assemble pertinent information, as well as formulate the best question, takes time and experience to learn.

There are numerous benefits of learning to ask power questions. You can expect to learn about the topic you're exploring. You'll learn about yourself, your abilities, and other people. You'll learn how to get what you want by asking powerful questions. You'll capture great answers and from them build new questions to help you uncover the details of your quest. You'll exercise your introspective muscle, which will give you a fine fitness level to not only discover, but actually get whatever you want in life.

How many times have you asked for something and not received it? Any ideas why that happens? Do you play word games like a volley of wit when you ask questions? For someone else, it can be confusing to know your game, and it likely won't get you the answer you need, because you need to ask a powerful question instead. What you want may be clear to you, but is it clearly comprehended by the one you're asking? How do you know if you've been understood?

You may ask, "How do I look?" But, do you actually mean, "Do I look fat in this?"

Asking, "What do you think about this?" is not as direct as saying, "What is your opinion of the current political situation regarding...?"

You may say, "Would you review my project?" But, what you really want to say is, "Can you sing praises for my work?"

We all ask for things haphazardly at one time or another. However, if you consistently approach your quest with this type of unclear questioning, beware of unmet expectations!

In a coaching situation, the coach's job is to help the client figure out her own dilemmas. The coach does this by carefully listening and repeating back to the client what she hears from the client. An effective coach has the knack to put this information into the context the client is ultimately asking for. This last part comes from the vast experience of a great coach. You, too, can learn some tricks to help yourself and the people around you, which will improve everyone's powerful quest!

"A good listener is not only popular everywhere, but after a while he knows something." - Wilson Mizner

Quality Listening is Like a Stereo with a High Quality Receiver

It doesn't feel like it was that many years ago that my husband bought a stereo system. It consisted of a set of rather huge speakers about the size of end tables, which they became. The turntable came next, and then the tape deck. The receiver was the key piece of equipment that all the rest was connected to by miles of wires. If you didn't have a good receiver, you wouldn't hear quality sound. It translated AM/FM radio, LP's, Cassette tapes, and eventually CD's. The receiver was the brains of the operation. It contained an amplifier; and every sound wave passed through it on the way to the speakers. This set up also required a large bookshelf or another system called the entertainment center.

Watching him connect all the equipment to our entertainment system was a good show all by itself. Each piece had its own type of plug and calibration. The last part was the antenna, which started a deeper discussion about how much more of the living room would be sacrificed just to listen to a good tune.

"No, it can't go on the top of the curtains. How will we open them?"

"No, it can't stay thumbtacked to the wall." Where will we hang the pictures?"

"No, we can't leave the wires all over the floor. How will we vacuum?"

The part of this experience that always amazed me was the difference between listening to the quality of the sounds from this elaborately webbed system, as compared to the AM radio in my VW. What a difference the fine tuning made. I could feel the vibrations of the music in my bones, and I felt as if I was awakening something deeper and wiser within me.

Questioning is quite like this old stereo system. When you ask a direct, well-crafted question, you can connect with another person's receiver. Acting like a computer, this receiver sends electrical impulses along miles of wires translating your words into a response. Artfully arranging your requests will awaken your listener's brain, and you will connect on a cellular level and get what you want. This is powerful!

Nevertheless, make no mistake. If you don't calibrate and correctly connect to this receiver, you will not be tuned in. When you ask someone for something, use specific words that wake up your listener's brain.

"To raise new questions, new possibilities, to regard old problems from a new angle, requires creative imagination..." - Albert Einstein

Power Questions
Connect to the Listener's Intellect

Ordinary questions are very much like Neanderthal grunts.

Cave dwellers huffed at each other, reacting to whatever was in front of them. Intellectual communication wasn't necessary beyond fulfilling basic needs. Today, when we ask a poor question, we'll just get a reaction, too. Questions that don't elicit the listener's intelligence will only evoke a quick reply - not brainy, just minimal connection.

As modern human beings, we have a sound and hearing machine finely linked within our brain inputting what we hear, though we don't always use it. When we put our words together without much thought about the outcome we want, we get what we asked for — a poor response. We leave a serious and ignorant hole in our chitchat when we don't ask important questions.

Suggested thoughts are wishy-washy gibberish. Suggestions don't employ our human intellect in a direct, productive way. If you want something, you have to specifically ask for it. The longer you take to figure out how to say it, the more you will wait to get what you want. The trouble with an indecisive approach is that you risk losing out altogether. You can be brushed off, quickly dispatched, or intensely engaged, all by the way you initiate your quest.

Our animal relatives communicated with grunts and howls. This bawling eventually became our language, full of words and deeper understanding. Now we can ponder the meaning of our existence instead of just surviving it. So what's the difference between primitive yowling and asking clear, concise questions?

Asking direct and specific questions creates a powerful connection between the main computers of individual human brains. Talking to someone is different from talking at them. Peripherally gesturing toward another human being dismisses the miracle of our creative potential. What a waste! There is so much we can be a part of when we bother to truly communicate.

Our brains are quite amazing in the way they open and close our thoughts. Most often, our minds are surfing for something really meaty to engage. Much of the time, we're dealing with mediocre input, so when something lively comes along, our brains jump start our innovative systems. When asked a really great question, we get stimulated.

As a creative person, I often wonder if living through a human life is actually just about asking a bunch of questions. Perhaps it's the modern life we live, full of technical advantages, which has created so many more questions than answers. At our fingertips, we have access to the world. We can find any tidbit of information about everything we can imagine. We walk around with the tools that give us the ability to be wise. However, none of this miracle technology works without asking the best questions. So, I suspect what differentiates us from the rest of the animal kingdom, is that we're yearning to learn through our questions.

"I'm not a genius. I'm just a tremendous bundle of experience." - R. Buckminster Fuller

Power Questions Connect Us in Emotional, Intuitive Ways

I asked a bunch of my friends and associates two questions in order to find examples of actual people using powerful questions. The answers to their quests revealed how they were able to engage another person and receive what they wanted to know. The two questions are:

#1. What's the best question you've ever asked?

#2. What's the best question ever asked of you?

No surprise, most responded with more questions.

"Do you mean practical questions or higher level questions?"

"How much time do I have to answer?"

"Can I answer as a writer or from under one of the other hats I wear?"

"Are you going to talk about the best answers?"

"Are you open to anything?"

You see, when you initiate a quest, people love the engagement!

Life does seem to be a series of questions. Some lead to stories and engage our interest through emotions. Read this answer from Jaqueline, a fellow artist:

What's the best question you've ever asked?

"I took a class with a famous artist who introduced painting fish by saying, 'Paint what you know, and it will be simplified.' He was adamant that we should all try painting fish the way he did it. I asked him, 'What do I know about painting fish?' He said, 'Keep trying.' I painted a few more that day, and in the morning he left a Post-it note on my painting that said, 'Stop painting fish!' I went to him and asked, 'Why?' And he said,

'I don't need the competition!' I took that to mean that my fish were pretty good!"

All questions lead to connections. Some we may not wish to continue, and others we will. This response came from a friend who works in a call center:

"Okay, most of my stuff is pretty scripted. But, one day, I asked a man, who was from Tennessee and who had an unusual name, if he was related to an obstetrician in my home town. He said that would be his father, who was the doctor who delivered all my brother's kids. Small world."

Sometimes, our quest just takes us in an entirely different direction. My request for answers to my questions prompted this response from Cecily, a friend:

"Is there something going on cosmically?"

When we're looking for specific information, we ask questions. My friendly photographer Susan shared these answers:

"I attended a presentation put on by the local camera store about five years ago. A well-known photographer, who travels via airplanes extensively, gave a presentation. Since I have never flown with my equipment, I asked him how he packed and carried his equipment when flying. The info that I received about traveling on planes and packing was very helpful."

"I was with a friend in Colorado, and as we were hiking along a lakeside trail, he asked me if I get more of a thrill of having my photography published, or of licensing the images for publication."

There might be something contagious about asking good questions because it seems to promote a quest in others. How many times have you heard someone answer one question with another?

"What do you want to eat?"

"I don't care. What do you want?"

Sometimes, this viral questing is productive, and great innovations find their way to life. Other times, too many questions cause congestion and confuse the intended focus. This is why the ability to ask really powerful questions is one of humankind's greatest assets.

Can you imagine the questions asked in Thomas Edison's laboratory throughout the process of 10,000 light bulb failures and the one magical success? Do you suppose there were days of utter confusion? Days where the important process was to figure out the most powerful questions, and then answer them?

So why don't we exercise our ability to ask really great and powerful questions?

One emotional reason we don't feel comfortable asking questions is that it can make us feel vulnerable to not know something. Adults play games with themselves around feeling exposed, letting their wonder drift off into a belief that there could be another way, like a magical osmosis to discover what we need without touching risk and asking great questions. Questing is all about discovery; and discovery won't exist without asking questions. The better your questions, the more superior your discoveries, and the further enhanced will be your value, leading to a much richer personal wisdom.

You can ask powerful questions!

I'm well educated, and I bet you are, too. I have academic degrees and numerous certifications. Moreover, there are my life long experiences, the sum of which have given me so much more than textbooks and classrooms, because that's where I tried out what I was taught. Real life is also where I figured out what actually works, as I imagine you, too, have found rich, value-laden wisdom from which to formulate your own great questions.

I could reference for you some well-crafted academic missives on this topic, but I'm not going to, because, first of all, I'm really glad you bought my book and are reading it — thanks from my heart! Second, I'm not sending you elsewhere, because I read many of those books, and while they're very good on their topics, I couldn't find a book about talking to regular folks in everyday language about how to ask power questions. That's my universe! I also know where we miss in our connections with one another. And it starts with the way we question.

"Without wonder and insight, acting is just a trade. With it, it becomes creation." -Bette Davis

Ask Your Questions from Your Place of Wonder

So what is it that makes us ask questions, really great questions? Both wonder and curiosity play an important part. You have to want to know something to formulate your thoughts around a question. I also believe that to put together a great question you need a bit of childlike surprise; a fragment of mystery that creates a nugget for your imagination to land on, and take root. A good story teller comes to mind here.

To tell a good story, you need to stimulate the emotions of your audience. You need to move them into your mind's eye with the words you choose. You must put them into the actionable feeling of what you're saying. It's the same when you're asking a good question. The marvel of what you sense needs to come across through your words and emotional tone. Children just bleat it out as they feel it. Their passion for their quests is palpable. Yours will be, too, so align your curiosity with that innocent and passionate part of you, and ask your questions from your place of wonder.

Wade, a friend, shared: "The best question I ever asked was: 'Tell me about your self-reflection; what brings you to the *A-ha* discovery?' The best question ever asked of me was of the same introspection."

Introspection! That's what we're really talking about! It makes a quest come alive. We're not just ordering cheeseburgers here. We're on an important journey through asking powerful questions.

Be a walking question mark. No, I don't mean to walk hunched over. What I mean, is to observe the world around you and figure out what questions you need and want to ask, and of whom and how you will ask them.

"Creativity, as has been said, consists largely of rearranging what we know in order to find out what we do not know. Hence, to think creatively, we must be able to look afresh at what we normally take for granted."- George Kneller

Power Questions Solicit Answers that Stimulate Introspection

Gaining real introspection takes time, and it's not a simple task. It speaks to change, which, whether we want to accept it or not, is always happening. It's difficult to accept new ideas, feelings, or possibilities. Asking questions, formulated for truly hearing what is being said, brings a client into the position to know and feel parts of her being that she may not yet know or understand.

We need to be seen and heard in order to feel we are connected to other people. We need each other for introspective peeks. This may seem a bit odd, but it is how every one of us makes self-improvement. We shift habits when we can see and understand them from a different perspective. We must step back to take a look at where we are. Only then can we come to know who we are.

Asking, "How am I doing?" is a powerful question. However, it's meaningless without a true introspective evaluation. When we understand our deepest parts, we can begin to shift into the being we want to be. As a coach, I sometimes feel like the good question fairy. I wave my wand and powerful questions float out; or, so many of my clients seem to think. It's not entirely true of course. What I do is hear their words and feel their emotions. Then I turn those same words and emotions back on them through questions so they can explore more fully what, deep down, they already know intuitively they want. That's my magic!

One day, deep into my own writing, while putting this manuscript into its final draft, I felt a bit lost. I fought off the strong urge to blow off my schedule and go out and do something else, even though that felt as though it would be easier and more fun to do. One of the benefits of being a creativity coach is I understand the landscape of creating, and this type of distraction can kill a creative project. Every time I plowed through my draft, the thought of wanting to be a better wordsmith kept tossing through my mind. I would have felt so much more pleasure to go out and smell the roses, to just be elsewhere.

To create, you have to show up and do the work. Bored, scared, and feeling stupid, I pressed on. I wrote words and phrases that seemed witty enough, but I knew my passion was off trying to have a good time in some other place. Real bummer for me! The truth, though, is a finished product isn't all glamour and praise. In fact, most of it is sweaty and critical. I don't mean it's all suffering, though some artists do suffer a lot. What I mean, is that real work is just that - work. It's full of setbacks, new learning, exploration, and perspiration. There is a physical investment partnered with time that must take place. It's the incubation of the created idea. It has to grow and become something of form and substance so we can share its experience.

Most perplexing to me, on this day, was the innate self-knowledge that I really needed my passion to help me create the important questions, which ultimately would initiate the decisions I needed to make creating this final draft. Boy was I stuck. I committed to get this work finished by a specific date on a specific timeline. Publication loomed before me, and all I wanted was to take a trip anywhere out of here! A story from my past brushed across my mental screen and reminded me, I needed a fresh approach to formulate the power questions that would get my writing of this book unstuck. Without leaving my desk, I needed to go on a quest to get back into my writing groove.

Quite a few years ago, I healed from a nasty childhood. My healing process was metaphoric, full of asking hard questions and searching for their answers. I learned a lot about asking powerful questions during this time. I wrote a memoir of my experience, and this excerpt came to mind as I felt stuck with my writing.

A Fish Out of Water

The sun was hot, the day had a breeze. The books the head nun gave me talked of betrayals. And, I lay on that pier for hours reading the trashy truth of my life. I felt as if the authors knew more about my existence than I did. How? It wasn't obvious to me. I thought I knew it all already. Driven, I lay there getting more burnt by the minute, not sure if it was the sun overhead or the inferno of rage boiling within me searing my skin. The surrounding cool water beckoned me, "Just end this."

As I lay full of thought, motionless, feeling the pull deep beneath the water and a sick sensation in the pit of my stomach, I began to confront a painful powerful choice. Suddenly, inches from my face, a fish jumped out of the water!

Startled, my mind began to race with different thoughts. I wondered if this fish wanted to die, too. Was it in pain? What makes a fish jump out of water anyway? Why would it leave its safe world? Maybe it wasn't secure there, just like I wasn't safe growing up.

My mind snapped into high gear. Now, my own deep thoughts interrupted and irritated, I really wanted to know what makes a fish jump out of water. It can't breathe for long out of water. It can't live, but if it wanted to die, why didn't it just jump on land?

I don't remember how many fish jumped up out of the water that afternoon, but a whole mess of them did. Every time my thoughts drifted back into slipping away, down into the quiet, cool depths of that lake — a damn fish jumped up and out! Some of them actually splashed my face with that cold water. They eventually garnered my entire attention, and I was intrigued by them. What were they doing? There were no flying bugs to be eaten. Now, I'm sure a biologist would have some scientific explanation, but I was on a magical life journey that week, and these jumping fish were my omen.

Finally, it occurred to me, maybe they were trying to get a look at me? But why take that risk? Wouldn't a fish think a human might eat them? Wouldn't they be afraid to see what might happen to them? Why leap to another realm where you'll be breathless in an instant? Why take a look at something so scary?

Feeling perhaps they were just looking at the whole picture of who they were and where they came from — it hit me. I too, was a fish out of water, gasping for air, risking my security to get a glimpse of a new perception of my life. I, too, was taking a chance to rise above and see the whole picture; to see the truth.

After I reread this piece, I decided to include it here as an example of how seemingly ridiculous and random events can collide, giving us something quite valuable. Golden treasures that change lives are all around us if we look to see them. They are part of the magic that a truly powerful set of questions can have.

So what did I do with this reminder that I needed a new perspective? How did I call my passion back into my work? No, I didn't run away. I decided to use a simple Play Strategy, one that gave me some joy while doing my work. How could I make this particular writing phase fun?

I chose to spend no more than an hour downloading new music to inspire me. And, it worked. No more fish out of water on this book!

To summarize, so far we've discussed Strategies:

1. Know what you want to get.
2. Know what you're willing to negotiate.
3. Get responses, not reactions.
4. Use HALOS.

Chapter Three Summary Power Questions

How do you know what you want from your power quests?

How do you decide what you want to negotiate, in order to get what you want?

What changes might you make in your line of power questing to get real and helpful responses?

How will using HALOS specifically help you in your power quests?

Chapter Four

Going on a Quest — What's Your Tale?

"To be on a quest is nothing more or less than to become an asker of questions."

-Sam Keen

I don't know if it's the bane of cell phones, but, as a culture, our speech is getting rotten. We don't ask good questions, yet we expect everyone else knows how to figure out our answers. We assume. We suspect. We don't listen. We yak on and on and on. We miss valuable human connection. In fact, we crave it, but many just don't have a clue how to find it through conversation. Being able to craft a powerful question so you can get a great response is a necessary skill that will help you navigate your world successfully.

You've probably overheard a loud cell phone conversation by a stranger. Could you make sense of it? Did it seem both parties were actually communicating, or were they talking in circles? Perhaps you've also heard what I call simultaneous conversations, because it appears people are not even talking to each other. They don't listen; instead, they just react to whatever they're thinking at the moment.

It takes two sides for a dialogue to occur. A good talk is like a well-choreographed dance. One person leads and the other follows. During a good conversation, the participants reverse their roles often. A fluid movement begins the process of chatting between two people, with both of them gaining and giving information. The more you know someone, the easier it will be for the verbal waltz to take place. The less you know someone, the more you need to have good questioning skills.

We discover, claim, explore, thrill, desire, grow, create, and love through asking the best questions. In any good exchange of information, the person on her quest issues an invitation to her audience to interact through interviewing with powerful questions. There are many ways to make a great quest powerful. The 17 Strategies are helpful principles you can use to explore human connections, in order to fulfill your need to accrue knowledge.

I've written this book as a coach for professional coaches, managers, and other creators dealing with the need to answer questions, but it can easily adapt to any other professional field (chiropractor, teacher, doctor, lawyer, plumber, automotive technician, supervisor, or anyone in customer service). You can use your own title interchangeably with coach. And it definitely will help you communicate in your personal relationships, too.

Being Present with Clients as They Decide Their Quests

Tom Thumb, Peter Pan, and Thumbelina all went on many quests. Each had varied experiences along the way. But none of them found what they wanted until they decided what that desire was to be. Thumbelina was to marry and enter into a relationship that would make her unhappy until she decided happiness was her desire. Then her prince appeared. The boys, Tom and Peter, went on numerous adventures with abandon, succumbing to near escapes because their quests were not thoughtful.

In my professional experience, when people have trouble with life matters, their careers, or creativity, most of the time they are not asking the right questions. The rest of the time, they just don't bother to ask anything. The most important part of asking the right question is to make it the most powerful question you can.

My clients come into coaching sessions to find answers. Though I don't have answers for them, I do have a process that helps them find their own solutions and make their best choices. I "quest" to ask the best questions I can, and, by doing so, I help them discover their own secrets and truths.

One of my clients summed up being coached by me this way: "It's like having someone present with you in everything you do." She learned that when I coached her, much of what I could help her through, came from asking the important questions. She already knew most of her own answers, and so do most of my clients. Since I don't give them answers, my clients quickly figure out our journey together is one of their own introspection, and I'm along to take careful notes and pop in with the questions that need to be asked.

How you form your questions will elicit different kinds of answers. If you ask whether a person wants to do something specific, for example, work on her book, she will answer with a yes or no. If you instead ask what she wants to do about writing her book, you will get some interesting information. But, for more workable details, you will need to format your question in a definitive fashion. Asking "What is your plan to write your book?" will be more to the point and yield a more specific answer than asking, "Do you want to write your book?" in regards to addressing the issues confronting the writer.

Effective Coaching Through Dialogue

For coaching to be effective, clients need to enter into a dialogue about what they want to accomplish. It's up to the coach to devise a route of questioning that illuminates the client's facts, truths, values, desires, abilities, willingness, opportunities, and choice. It's the same process for managers, creative thinkers, or anyone trying to solve a problem.

Trust is imperative in getting a good response. Trust can have many forms. You may think of it as only used to make a conversation comfortable, but trust can also be used as a guarantee, like when a client feels assured she will be able to continue to work on her goals because the coach consistently shows up ready to help her. If you ask your questions in such a way as to create trust, your client will feel safe and know you mean business. Then you'll get your desired response.

Here's a sample of a conversation that includes several approaches to growing a dialogue:

"Would you like to learn to paint?"

"Yes."

"What would you paint?"

"My bedroom."

"Oh, I meant paint in oils on a canvas."

"Yeah, I might like that, too, but I need to paint my bedroom."

"What color would you paint your bedroom?"

"Lavender."

"Why Lavender?"

"Because it's supposed to be relaxing."

"Do you want to relax more?"

"Yes!"

At this point, all you know is that your client feels they need to relax and they're planning to paint their bedroom in lavender, a color they hope will help calm them.

Here's another approach:

"How are you feeling in this moment?"

"Rushed, overwhelmed, tired..."

"Are you stressed? Yes."

"What is overwhelming you?"

"My work, my partner, my friends, school..."

I don't ask questions just to get reactions. As a creativity coach, my job is all about forming questions that will tease out different kinds of responses. Why? Because, as a coach, I look for a client's responses and repeat them back to the client as powerful statements, reflecting the client's truth like breath on a mirror.

We all yearn to be witnessed and heard in decisive ways. We're different in our individual notable manner, so as a coach, I look for the important details that spell out who each client is and what their purpose is all about. If you manage or provide a service to other people, you'll want to do the same. The way I formulate my questions creates the foundation of my coaching practice and my relationships with my clients.

Many elements go into our communication. It's true all animals share some form of communication. Some even utilize parts of their brain to analyze the information and use it for their benefit. There are monkeys in Africa that have figured out if they sound the alarm for snake, the rest of the monkeys will scatter for cover, giving them the chance to steal the food they want. They must have been on a learning quest at some point in their evolution in order for them to have figured out that crying wolf changes the playing field for their favor.

Human beings differ from other species in the way we communicate. We question a lot. We use our questions to explore our thoughts about everything in our universe, from the cars we drive to the stars we watch. We wonder and most important — we create. Which is one of the reasons why, as a creativity professional, I'm writing this book about power questions. They intrigue me, because they're the foundation of creative expression.

A good quest is full of insightful questions yielding rich answers. If you work with a coach, you probably understand what I mean. If you don't yet work within a coaching model, I think you'll be pleasantly surprised by the process. Imagine having a friendly person witnessing your adventures and helping you extricate the important parts?

What magical things could you create with a relationship like this? How could you feel failure when you have someone there to call out the wonder of your lessons? Someone who positively captures the essence of what it is like to be the worst and the very best you?

I think one of the scariest things we can face is to feel all alone. Working with a coach busts that feeling. Coaches are available in all specialties to help you explore living the best life you choose. They help you recognize your different parts. A great coach doesn't tell you what to do, they help you discover it — in your own way!

How to Make a Great Quest Powerful

"How do you know so much about everything?' was asked of a very wise and intelligent man; and the answer was 'By never being afraid or ashamed to ask questions as to anything of which I was ignorant."-John Abbott

What makes a great quest powerful? When you ask questions that matter, personalize your questions, pay attention to your manner and tone, match emotion to the client or person you're questioning, and tap into your passion and energy as you seek answers, you will garner powerful results.

You can ask questions about anything; however, to have a great quest, you'll need to think about what is important so you can formulate the questions that matter. You'll also need to think about what resources you want to tap and who the people are who have the responses that matter to you. This is where *Strategy 10, Recognizing Differences*, will come in handy.

Personalizing your requests creates an experience for both you and the person you're asking. It's a wonderful way to connect, and it will expand the scope of your adventure.

> "Sally, I know you have dabbled in acrylic paints. Do you have any suggestions for what particular yellow works best to represent the setting sun?"

The way you ask for information will determine the type and the depth of response you get. Your tone will speak to your passion, telling your audience the level of your sincerity and your desire to have them participate.

> "Derek, I know that you've recently lost your job, and this isn't the first time you have faced these challenges, so how do you want to proceed using your wisdom?"

> "Lily, I just love the way you write, and I'm wondering if you are interested in teaching what you know to a grade school class of kids?"

When you match your own emotion to that of your listener's, you can immediately connect on the same level. This will make it easier for both of you to explore your topic.

> "Bob, you're writing is so emotional and really touches upon the human side of gentleness. Have you considered publishing any of your poems?"

> "Jane, I feel your distress, what can we accomplish together today?"

Don't be afraid to share your passion for what you want. We all love to see each other light up with what inspires us. When you watch a friend who is truly excited about something, they seem to come alive, and it feels good to share in their happiness. Showing your energy for a project is equally important for a great quest. It lets your listeners know you're serious and enthusiastic about your exploration.

> "Hi Dan, how are you doing with that novel of yours? I can't wait to read the first draft. I loved your last story. It really touched my sensibilities and helped me see another perspective."

> "Suzie, I especially look forward to your next pottery show. Your last show had so many interesting items. You have a special knack to add whimsical notes to your work. It makes your show a fun experience."

For those of you who are reading this book in a strictly professional manner, I want to add a quick note about setting appropriate professional relationship boundaries. Depending on your specific situation, you may not be actually reading manuscripts or attending art shows, because it creates a more casual and possibly interpersonal relationship. Becoming involved in commenting on a client's work entails a different type of communication, one that is more like a consultant, a service provider who does give advice in the form of answers, would use, rather than a coach.

You can easily adapt this type of personalized question for the corporate world, too.

> "Molly, I really appreciated your last report. You were able to address the issues and include some human touches that made it easy to understand and adapt. Could you explain your method to our advertising team?"

I've done a lot of coaching for consultants, and one of the things they often get confused about is how their clients engage with all the information they're trying to explain. Since there are many different audiences that are addressed in any major corporate or public project, there will be numerous ways of assimilating the information. Chunking down the information and tailoring it to the specific audiences, along with using language and methods they are used to dealing with, usually does the trick.

Engineers speak in a specific way and like to deal with facts and figures. Policy makers like to deal with popular favor and trends over what seems practical. Consumers are very emotional, but will also radically change opinions based on finances.

My favorite consultant summed up his two questions this way:

1. What's the best question you've ever asked?

   "What information do you need to make a decision?"

   "How do you know?"

2. What's the best question asked of you?

   "Why should I/We pick you?"

   "How do you know?"

You can see by these answers that asking specific questions that get to the point and inspire the client to think will help the project move along. Having her explain how she got to her current understanding will tell you a lot about the process she used. A good consultant, coach, or manager can use this knowledge to ascertain what the client knows and the pools of information available to her. By using specific questions, the consultant is able to gather and evaluate pertinent client information and then decide where additional resources might be needed.

In this chapter, we've discussed what makes a great quest powerful. Going on a quest is an important journey you must navigate; and recognizing the value of differences will help you find your way. I've given a few more examples about the importance of being clear and concise, and how to be direct when asking your question.

The Strategies illustrated in this chapter are:

1. Be clear and concise.
2. Recognize differences.
3. Navigate and be a navigator.
4. Use HALOS

Chapter Four Summary Power Questions

What are some of your requirements for engaging in a great quest?

Where do you find your inspiration for powerful questions?

What helps you recognize differences that you need to pay attention to?

What helps you navigate your quests?

What quests require you to be the navigator?

What makes a great quest powerful?

In what quest situations would HALOS help you most?

Chapter Five

Listening —
If Little Red Riding Hood
Had Paid Attention...?

"Listening looks easy, but it's not simple. Every head is a world."

-Cuban Proverb

Listening is a magical skill; and not because it seems some people do it regularly and many others don't. I believe in its magic because listening opens the hearts of others. Listening stimulates every individual like a flower opens to the morning light. Dew kissed and ready, that flower engages the elements surrounding it. The wind shakes it so it will know its strength. The sun bakes it, rendering the colors that mark it an individual. Alive with the energy of witness, that single flower expresses its beauty, serving its purpose.

People are like that flower. When we are listened to, we are as appreciated as the brilliance that flower exudes in its moment of glory. We are ripe for the picking when we are heard, because being witnessed is glorious for our soul. Our spirit ignites with the joys of being alive when we are appreciated; and being noticed invites us to imbibe in the sweet nectar of human interconnection.

"When people talk, listen completely. Most people never listen." -Ernest Hemingway

Listening is a natural skill we teach to our young by hearing them and inviting them to life by asking questions about their thoughts. We educate each other through our questions and the ways in which we listen.

If Little Red Riding Hood had listened carefully, might she have discovered the wolf wearing her grandmother's clothes and saved herself from being eaten? In the original version, she was dinner. Had she used her powers of observation, this tale would have ended differently. If you want to have a good experience and successful quest, you'll need to pay close attention to everyone involved.

Can you describe the way your grandmother talked? What emotions prevailed in her words? Can you clearly tell how you're loved ones perceive their day's journey? Do you know how they want to build their future? What inspires their manner of speech? Can you pinpoint what they most desire from a single day? How well do you listen for the little things that spell each individual you encounter? How can you engage these special details and open that individual to sharing a moment in her life with you?

> "Listening is a magnetic and strange thing, a creative force. The friends who listen to us are the ones we move toward. When we are listened to, it creates us, makes us unfold and expand." - Karl Menninger

The Pause

I know when I've helped my client get into a touchy area of her work, because the power question gives a moment of pause. Literally, she gasps and spits air for a brief time before the brain kicks in. At this moment, the client almost always knows we have hit the mark, and this targeted question opens the crux of the day's matter. Then my job is to listen carefully for what the client says next. Her words usually dictate the next round of questions to follow, and the tone that will help.

Often clients ask and answer a set of questions that bring them to a different level. Capturing their words during this time is extremely helpful to you, the coach, because when you frame your questions using their own words, the quest becomes a powerful experience for your clients.

One goal I work toward is to create the *pause*. What do you do with a *paused* moment? As a coach, it signals me to actively pay attention and listen carefully. It's imperative I step off the path and let my client explore this particular stretch of earth, traversing her way over the logs and rocks along the journey she's exploring. What the client needs most is for me to hold space open for her to experience her stumbling about.

This moment can be difficult for the interviewer. It feels natural to fill in a paused dialogue. It's been dubbed the "pregnant pause" because we tend to feel uncomfortable when no words are spoken while many thoughts are felt. Yet, we have a strong sense something needs to happen. Take heed, this is exactly the moment a coach works to create. It is not the time to share other analogies, information, or experiences. Be silent and *hear with all your senses*. Gather all the little details of your client's expression, or lack of. Take note of her speech patterns and all the small shifts that occur. Feel her emotions.

If you're going to ask the best question to find the best response, you'll need to get comfortable with the *pause* in your dialogues. Practice getting calm and silent and just observing what goes on around you. You can also practice holding the *pause* in your own conversations, by not speaking fast and pausing for a moment before you say anything.

I also believe it's valuable to develop the skillset of receiving the information revealed in a *paused* moment. You can do this by calming your own thoughts and feelings; and, then detach from them while you hear what is being said. Remember, you'll need to feed back what you are hearing, so you'll need to also practice repeating exactly what you heard.

"So, I heard you say, that you would like to open a coffee shop because you want to feel like you are helping people in little ways every day. Is that correct?"

"An essential part of true listening is the discipline of bracketing, the temporary giving up or setting aside of one's own prejudices, frames of reference and desires so as to experience as far as possible the speaker's world from the inside, step in inside his or her shoes. This unification of speaker and listener is actually an extension and enlargement of ourselves, and new knowledge is always gained from this. Moreover, since true listening involves bracketing, a setting aside of the self, it also temporarily involves a total acceptance of the other. Sensing this acceptance, the speaker will feel less and less vulnerable and more and more inclined to open up the inner recesses of his or her mind to the listener. As this happens, speaker and listener begin to appreciate each other more and more, and the duet dance of love is begun again." - M. Scott Peck, MD

Before you set out on an interview quest, it will serve you to remember what you hope to gain from your questions. People willingly talk about the things that energize them. So sensing the energetic nature of your client is important.

"What would make you excited to get up early tomorrow?"

"What do you do that really inspires you?"

"What parts of this project give you a thrill?

"How can you make this a fun and exciting adventure?"

"You have to be willing sometimes to listen to some remarkable bad opinions. Because if you say to someone, 'That's the silliest thing I've ever heard; get on out of here!'—then you'll never get anything out of that person again, and you might as well have a puppet on a string or a robot." - John Bryan

Respect

"To say that a person feels listened to means a lot more than just their ideas get heard. It's a sign of respect. It makes people feel valued." - Deborah Tannen

You can't be a good listener if you have no respect for the process or the people involved in your conversation. Asking respectful questions is another part of my coaching formula. I'd like to believe this is just common sense, and everyone will know what I'm talking about, right? Maybe not; let's be real about this. I have my reality, and you have yours. That's good. It's supposed to be this way. And because it is this way, common sense may not provide respect, because we all operate from our own set of standards.

Dangerous Assumptions

"Effective listeners remember that 'words have no meaning - people have meaning'. The assignment of meaning to a term is an internal process; meaning comes from inside of us. And although our experiences, knowledge and attitudes differ, we often misinterpret each other's messages while under the illusion that a common understanding has been achieved." - Larry Barker

People talk at one another all the time. Let's listen in for a moment.

"Hi! How are you?"

"Fine. How are you?"

"I'm OK. What have you been up to? I haven't seen you for a while."

"Oh, I've been busy doing the same old stuff."

"Yeah, I know what you mean. Me, too."

"Well, nice to see you and catch up."

"Yeah, you too. Stay in touch."

Really? Do they know what each other is talking about? I doubt it. They're both off in their own assumptions of what is being communicated, but no real communication is taking place. They've just made noise in the other's direction. I'm not even sure this counts as connection, because nothing meaningful connected. We speak at each other like this often, with little gain.

A power quester knows different. She knows she'll have to do the important detective work of posing better questions. She understands that to connect she has to go for a serious response, and not settle for reactions.

"The way to stay fresh is you never stop traveling, you never stop listening. You never stop asking people what they think." - Rene McPherson

People talk at one another, asking unclear questions, and then make those dangerous assumptions that the other folks will know what the heck they want. It's downright foolish of you to expect someone to understand what you're saying, much less asking, if you can't state it clearly. To talk plainly, you need to know how to listen.

Listen in:

"Do you know a good restaurant around here?"

"Bill's Barfateria."

"The Barfy Bar and Grill."

"Yackups."

"Café Croak."

I can think of a thousand answers to this one. How many can you come up with? The truth is, you'll need to ask for more information in order to get a good recommendation for your meal.

- What do you like to eat?
- What do you want to eat?
- What do you need to eat?
- When are you planning on eating?

Let's learn the formula every great coach uses to fulfill a good human connection, building trust, through asking the powerful question.

You need to tease out your dialogue by carefully crafting your line of questioning. If you want to get responsive answers, you're going to need to ask unambiguous questions. Always respect and consider your audience. Form your questions with these three rules as often as possible.

The Great Coaches Quest Formula

- Be Simple
- Be Unmistakable
- Be Consistent

Get to the point quickly. Use words most people can understand. Remove the mental clutter that exists in everyone's mind by speaking as few words as necessary to make your point. The less your listener has to sort through, the easier it will be for her to respond to your request. Keep your questing simple.

Stop confusion before it starts by speaking clearly. Don't add extra information to your questions. Hidden agendas just bamboozle your focus. Adding more facts than are necessary to ask for the response you want, only makes your quest harder. To reach a good result, be unmistakable.

Be constant as you ask your questions. If you don't get the response you're looking for, ask it again. The best course is to repeat exactly what you said, several times. Our human nature has a nasty habit of changing our words when we repeat them. Say your words exactly as you first spoke them. If you don't, you'll be adding more information and changing the question. This leads to frustration and uncertainty. Remember you are operating based on trust. Don't give up. Be persistent. After a few repeats, your audience will signal about the part they don't understand. Listen for this carefully and only then restate your question differently, remaining constant in your focus.

I don't like blind followers. If I've exposed my own edginess in this comment, well, so be it. There are certain things that drive me nuts, or I wouldn't be a human being. We need our preferences and biases to define who we are, how we are, where we are, when we're there, and, to a larger degree, why we are. This last one, *why we are*, is perhaps the most important and least pondered. *Why are you?* Completely existential in nature, this question is worthy of an ongoing, lifelong dialogue. *Why are YOU?* In coaching, this is a great question that leads to many other amazing discoveries. Answering it leads to the core of one's intrapersonal meaning and life purpose.

Finding out what a person believes about themselves is a revealing and often scary awareness; however, in the caring hands of a skilled coach, the experience can be a beautiful opportunity, too juicy to ignore.

Many books beg answers to questions about who you are. Some are certainly better at it than others; yet, most of the ones I've read seem to talk at you. Rather than ask clear questions about me that I can find answers to, I often get the impression the authors think they know something about me that I don't. I doubt they actually do, so why quest with me in that way? Why not just ask unambiguous questions and let me ponder clear cut answers? Conversations, whether internal, like when reading a book, or with a real person, are all enriched by forming questions that elicit something worth listening for.

Paying attention to what the client says is the crucial secret of an expert coach. She practices until she's really skilled at listening. If you can't listen, you're not in a dialogue, and you'll miss most of the important communication around you. To truly hear what a person is saying, you'll need to follow:

The Great Coaches Listening Credo

- First and foremost, use your ears

- Next, open your mind

- Last, use your mouth - only to clarify what you heard

In my coaching practice, I'm careful to distinguish between asking a client, "Who are you?" from asking them, "Why are you?" Timing is certainly a part of when to pose the latter question, but after I ask, I get the heck out of the way — and listen deeply. The getting out of the way part is another very important skill of a great coach, or any other professional who's on a quest to learn about someone.

Hold aside your personal material so you can be present and hear what is being laid before you. Your client is sharing thoughts that are intrinsically valuable, and you're being trusted to hold, touch, caress, look at, love, like, or manage all, in order to reflect them back to the client in a safe and honorable manner. How you phrase and ask your questions will tell her how you are handling her intrapersonal treasure chest.

Envision this for a moment: Your client hands you her hat. Now, in your hands, it feels rough and a bit sweaty. You can see it is well worn, and you think it's tacky and should be thrown away. The longer you hold it, the more you feel the stickiness on your hands. You feel you want to drop the hat because you ___ (fill in the blank with any number of personal reactions).

Now envision this scenario, instead: You spend a few moments clearing your mind and placing your own thoughts and feelings aside before your client comes into your office. The client hands you her hat. You notice it is rough, sweaty, and well worn. You look at the client and ask, "How does your hat reflect where you are in this moment?" Then, you listen.

In the first example, too much of the coach's personal material was in the mixture and true hearing wasn't possible because of the coach's judgments. Personal bias doesn't really belong in a coaching session, but I'm going to define this in a specific way. We must have our bias. However, we need to manage it so it is used at the best point in the process. Sometimes, that means we must move on to other clients because we can't be of genuine service to the one we feel the need to judge. It's simply about making sure our own values are in sync with what we feel we can do for our clients, and that their values are in agreement. Otherwise there is the space for a mess to accumulate in the relationship.

It takes practice to be present and capable of listening to another speak, and it is worth the effort!

The Strategies we touched on in this chapter are:

1. Listen carefully and without letting your emotions interfere.

2. Hold your own character and characterizations back.

3. Stay focused.

4. Be patient.

5. Recognize differences.

6. Be creative and playful.

Chapter Five Summary Power Questions

What are your greatest difficulties when you need to listen carefully?

What helps you listen to someone speaking to you?

How does the skill of listening help you in your profession or creativity?

With what part of your body do you feel yourself hearing the message when someone is speaking to you? Does this differ depending on what is said?

Who is the best listener you know? How do you know they hear you?

What can you begin to do now that will help you listen deeper?

Chapter Six

You Can't Plant Magic Beans to Get What You Want —Where do Power Questions Originate?

"New opinions often appear first as jokes and fancies, then as blasphemies and treason, then as questions open to discussion, and finally as established truths."

- George Bernard Shaw

I've been groomed with plenty of experience in creativity, play, and the opportunity of effective communication. However, I discovered I've also used my other talents to aid my quests. I struggled for a while with the concept of this book and why I wanted to write about this topic. Sorting through my life, I realized I wanted to define something about myself through the creation of this manuscript.

I spent loads of time evaluating myself, my experiences, how others know me, what I learned from all my mistakes, and where I am now in my life in order to craft my thoughts. It's been a thrilling ride full of adventure, defeat, spontaneity, deep breaths, and you guessed it - powerful questions.

Writing a book is a spectacular quest; however, you are not reading these words because I planted magic beans and they grew upward into the pages you cradle! Jack took a big risk and tried something unorthodox to solve his problems. It may only take you a few hours to read through this book, but be assured, it took years to write. A really good quest is most likely going to take some time to complete.

I'm known by many titles, nicknames, labels, and identities that facilitate describing who I am. Artist, writer, creativity and life purpose coach, Mom, my princess, sweetie, Sand, woman, boomer, seamstress, creative, silver-haired, red-haired, innovative, inspirational, magical, gardener, painter, nature lover, dog fanatic, gourmet cook, tea lover and aficionado, humorous, good natured, humble, honest, highly principled, a bit crazy, fearless, wise, blunt, gentle, and introspective. This last identity is what propelled me to write this book.

Each part of me filters into my process of asking powerful questions. I can formulate my quests from many perspectives because I have a wealth of opportunity to figure out whatever I want to know, do, or create. Through the years, because of my special work using playfulness as a creative tool, I've grown to embody what may be (or what many have) described as a play wizard. So, I have taken on the title "The Play Wizard" since it best describes me as a coach. Here's the magical connection: all of these descriptions of me, which I readily play with, are the basis for my introspection.

Oh, yeah, this is a really cool mystical side note about why I may have been born to ask questions — literally. My birth name is pronounced "How." No joking! I was given the name Sandy How! All of my life I wondered about the meaning of my name, and now it seems to fit my creative puzzle through writing this book about powerful questions. This might be an otherworldly concept for you, but it's absolutely true.

I've no doubt your story is just as mysterious, with its own magical twists. I'm sure you also could write a similar list of descriptors. Try this exercise for yourself. Write down all the words that describe you now or in the past. Ask friends and family for help, too. Then reflect on this list to find your strengths and the assets you automatically use when you formulate your own powerful questions. You might discover that throughout your entire life, you have been on a specific quest of your own. What are some of the powerful questions that have guided you along?

We may have been born for particular quests. We may not have been; rather, we'll instead randomly bump into them. Either way, we will go on quests. What are your strengths? Which of your characteristics most often gets in the way of you finding the responses you seek? What are the main questions that guide you daily?

Sensory Quests Reveal Your Traits

Great skills are everywhere, but the talent to find them is rare. So when you have to discover information, you'll need to exercise your questing muscle. You do this by digging deeper with the words you choose to make up your power questions and using your own life experiences as fodder to fuel feelings. What specific strengths have helped you explore what you've most needed in your life? How can you use your experience to ask powerful questions? What lessons have these areas of your life taught you?

- Your past
- Your present
- Your future
- What you've learned
- How you learned what you know
- How it's changed your life

Who were you when you were young? What did you play? What did you really like to eat? What songs rattled through your lips? What did your childhood smell like? What colors bring your past alive again? Asking someone specific questions based on their sensory memories can give you some truly amazing information.

You could ask, "What activities did you do when you were a kid?" You'd get some feedback about the games that were played or the different kinds of activities they did. Alternatively, you could explore your own senses and ask something like, "What do your knees or the palms of your hands remember about your childhood?" I'd have to answer this one by remembering all my skinned knees and chafed palms gained from attempting to ride my bike too fast or roller skating and hitting the brakes by using the grass along the sidewalk. That would remind me that, while far from a natural athlete, I was pretty good at climbing trees. In fact, I can still feel the bark in my hands just like when I pulled myself upwards among the branches. What all of this type of questioning brings to me is the story behind the question's response.

Exploring your sensory quests might change your questions about the present. They might sound something like this:

- What are you doing today? or What sounds are you aware of hearing? Where are you working? or How are you working today?

- What did you eat for breakfast? or How does your food taste today?

- What is exciting today? or What pleasures have you touched upon today?

- What have you completed today? or How do you feel about the day?

Here are examples of sensory pattern adjustments for questions about the future:

- What do you plan on accomplishing? or When today is done, where do you hope to be with regard to your work, mental state, or physical fitness?

- What would you like to hear? or What sounds do you want to hear tomorrow?

- How can you add more flavor to your day? or What tastes do you plan on experiencing?

What you learned, how you learned it, and how it changed you make you the special being you are. Reflecting on these unique attributes can give you a treasure chest from which to pull out your own experiential learning and apply it to the questions you ask. When you get down to the stories that go with your questions and their responses, you've hit gold.

Emotion Quests, Like Seeds, Flourish when Tended

"We do not grow by knowing all of the answers, but rather by living with the questions." - Max De Pree

The value of our stories lies in the way they explain us. Everyone has had numerous experiences that developed their character. Learning about them from each other creates an exchange of ideas that make up a great quest.

Emotions are also quite telling. Have you ever been in a seemingly mild-mannered conversation and the other person starts to cry? What just happened? Questioning someone about their feelings can sometimes be tricky, but it will usually enrich your communication. Feelings speak very loud at times, and they can be a boon to formulating powerful questions. Getting to the story of your quest and involving another person with which to share it is magical.

Listen in on a response I received from Bonnie who works in a collections department:

> "The most consistent question I get from week to week that isn't 'Do you have a payment plan?' is 'Do you know what time it is?' In particular, on Saturday morning, when I start at seven Central Time and call across the country, through the four time zones, at eight o'clock local, the earliest we can call, people get very irritated! So I say, 'Yes, I know what time it is, and, yes, I am allowed to call you at this hour, and if you have a cell phone with an East Coast area code and you are now living in California, and it is 5:00 am, sorry, but not my fault.(But I do hang up!)"

Obviously, our emotions reveal quite a lot about us and can trigger all sorts of power packed questions.

Emotions can also lead us into some fertile territory about our passions. I received these question responses from Jack, who's a musician:

What's the best question you've ever asked?

> "Who has inspired you the most in your music? Where do you sense your musical gift came from?"

What's the best question asked of you?

> "Tell me more about your passion for music...How/when did it start? Who influenced you? Who inspires you the most now?"

Power questions come from deep within your being. Tap into what you know or want to know. Let your feelings guide your exploration. Allow your passion and energy to infuse your journey and awaken your quest.

For most of us, our unique story is what we are constantly grooming. We grow and change, and to do so, we need to ask powerful questions about ourselves and the world we live in, or want to live in. We need to gain the cooperation of other people to help us. One of the most powerful parts of our being is our vulnerability. It's here in this fragile place where we can be broken that our heart is in its truest form. This is also the best place from which to formulate our most intimately powerful questions.

Getting the story from another person happens through questioning them, and by baring your soul, you level the field so they can feel comfortable doing the same. Senses, emotions, life experiences, all play an important part in where you find your original power questions.

In this chapter we discussed a bit of the following Strategies:

1. Know what you want.
2. Know the types of questions.
3. Be creative and playful.

Chapter Six Summary Power Questions

What are some of the most powerful questions that have guided you through your life?

What are some playful ways you can ask power questions using your emotions?

How can you combine your creativity with your experiences to manifest powerful questions?

Which of your senses offer you the most information when you power quest?

Which of your strengths helps you the most when you need to gain information about another person's feelings?

What's the best story you can tell a stranger to illustrate who and how you are?

Chapter Seven

Get Responses, Not Reactions — The Wisdom of the Third Little Pig

"The law of floatation was not discovered by contemplating the sinking of things, but by contemplating the floating of things which floated naturally, and then intelligently asking why they did so."

-Thomas Troward

So far, I've shared my thoughts from the point of view of a Creativity Coach and Play Expert. However, I have a bit more to offer you. I've also spent years continually working beside my husband in a communication consulting business. In fact, our specialty is emergency telecommunications. Talk about needing to get to the point! You'd be amazed at the confused communications we actually speak in an emergency; all the while believing we're making sense to everyone.

9-1-1 operators are trained to ask specific questions — important questions that weed through the panic that occurs during an emergency. We can't help panicking in the moment during such a traumatic ordeal. However, we can learn to communicate what we need to get the results we want, just like dealing with an anxiety attack is a very doable feat. Plan ahead and practice sharing your personal information, because, in an emergency, you'll need to answer the powerful questions asked of you.

One of the chief skills of any consultant is listening carefully. As my consultant husband likes to say, "I just listen and repeat back what I heard." He's right, because as you now know, when you are on a quest, listening is as important as formulating the questions. In the world of emergency telecommunications, there is much at stake; and lots of angles to know about, facts to consider and multiple interests to serve. There are many laws, user agreements, human resource and government regulations to employ in a good 9-1-1 service.

Contrary to commonly held beliefs, your emergency service isn't just *magically* sitting somewhere waiting to serve you. Their readiness is certainly the goal; however, it takes an enormous amount of careful planning, negotiations, a hefty budget and financial allocation, taxation, training, management, and equipment to be a functional service. Every one of these elements creates a giant quest!

Communicating all of this effort and the specific and timely steps needed to create it for the populace it serves is as much of the quest as is figuring out what is needed, and by when. Maintaining a 9-1-1 service is approximately the same amount of work as designing and building one. Asking great questions is exactly why the services of a good consultant are usually needed for this kind of undertaking. Creativity Coaching is much the same. However, it is designed to work on an individual scale. And, no matter who you are, the example of emergency services can help expand your understanding of a great powerful quest.

I've served for years as the Coach to the Consultants, helping our teams work through the questing process on a great number of projects. I've watched as clients struggle to say what it is they want; and come to grips with what they need. I've witnessed public outcry over poorly communicated decisions and misled impressions. Sometimes, instead of questing, agencies or the citizens they serve make assumptions; they are comprised of human beings after all. These assumptions can jump to premature conclusions and clog the flow of progress where a more careful quest might not; hence, the need for a good coaching session about asking the power questions!

Let's listen in on a 9-1-1 call example:

"City-County Emergency"

"Help, I need help. My son is crying, he's hurt."

"What's your address?"

"323 Blackbird Drive."

"323 Blackbird Drive."

"Is this a house?"

"No, Apartment 2."

"OK, did you say your son is hurt Ma'am?"

"Yes! He's crying...he fell."

"Where did he fall?"

"From a ladder. Hurry please."

"Where is he now?"

"In the back yard."

"Is he breathing OK?"

"Yes, please hurry."

"We're sending help. An ambulance is on the way. Stay on the phone with me, alright? Is he bleeding?"

"His bone is poking thru the skin... He's crying."

"Don't move him. Make sure he continues to breathe OK."

"Please hurry!"

"Paramedics are on the way. Can they get in the back?"

"Yes, hurry!"

"How old is your son?"

"Six"

"How did he fall?"

"He was climbing onto the roof."

"How tall is the roof?"

"Three stories, I guess. He's still crying!"

"Are you able to help him?"

"I don't know what to do!"

"I'll tell you...can you take the phone with you?"

"Help me, he's crying!"

"The ambulance will be there soon."

"I can hear the sirens..."

The point of this line of questioning is to gather the necessary facts quickly and accurately. It's extremely difficult, because the person who has this information is traumatized and needs to be carefully and expertly managed through the crisis. I say with *full compliments*, a well-trained 9-1-1 operator is an asset you will always want to highly pay. Their job is to ascertain what's happened, arrange for the appropriate services to arrive at the correct place, help manage the caller, and do this all as quickly as possible. These skilled operators may not always sound polite or caring because theirs' is a specific lifesaving quest. They must wade through fear and panic to claim the facts and save lives.

You may never have to answer and navigate an emergency call; however, you may need to make one in an emergency. You'll probably be more affected with panic than you realize. It will help you, and the situation, if you practice these things:

- Where is the emergency? Clearly state your address or the address where you are located. (With cell phones so commonly used to make emergency calls, remember the 9-1-1 operator may not automatically know this information. Calling from a landline, if possible, is always best.)

- Clearly state if anyone, and how many, are injured. Is the injured person breathing? Is the injured person bleeding? Is the injured person conscious?

- Can the emergency crew get to the injured person easily?

In the case of emergencies, you'll benefit from anticipating the response you need and preparing the answers to these questions. When you travel, make sure you know the address of where you're visiting, as well as the appropriate number to dial for help. Never assume help is just around the corner. Know what emergency services are available in the areas you're visiting. If you know you have a situation that will likely need care, be prepared with the information that is most useful, and share it with your fellow travelers.

Emergency calls are an extremely charged type of quest to experience, but they demonstrate the need to:

- Be clear

- Be precise

- Be persistent

"You can tell whether a man is clever by his answers. You can tell whether a man is wise by his questions." - Naguib Mahfouz

So what about the third little pig? Why was he so wise? Because he created the circumstance to get the response he wanted.

You can anticipate your own emergencies by thinking about the kinds of questions you'll need to answer and preparing your answers ahead of time. After natural disasters, people are faced with a barrage of questions to answer if they're left homeless. In addition to basic facts, they need to know specific information to get their lives back on track. Here's a sample of some of those questions:

What is your bank account number?

What is your credit card account number?

What is your home and car insurance policy numbers?

What is your doctor's phone number?

What is your healthcare insurance policy number?

What is the phone number of your insurance agent?

What are your family members' medical prescription numbers?

What is the likely nature of your emergency? How can you prepare for it? What are the questions for which you'll need accurate answers?

> "Judge others by their questions rather than by their answers." - Voltaire

Get Responses

Crafting questions to get to productive responses is an art. It is applicable to many fields of service. A chiropractor needs to know how your joints and bones are, but she also may need to understand what physical activities you've been up to lately. So simply asking a patient how they are feeling, won't get to the information you may need. Asking a patient, "What do you hope to get from this series of treatment?" will yield a much different answer from asking, "How do you feel today?"

Lately, I've noticed a trend that my caregivers (dentists, chiropractors, and doctors) have been more interested in what I did this weekend and during my off work hours. This does open a whole new conversation for us and provides more information that explains how I feel. My chiropractor has learned to read my bruises. I'm a bit of a klutz! She can tell how long ago I did something by their color. She knows to ask if I was painting or gardening, or more specific questions, in order to determine what I did to cause the bruising. She can also use this information to help me prevent injury by asking me what my plans are ahead of the coming weekend. Then she gives me reminders and tips of what I can do in a more proper way to maintain my health.

Coaching can be like this, too. We can become investigators, searching out little details that illustrate our clients' lives. Then we can help them make small adjustments through posing appropriate questions based on their specific needs.

> "So, tell me Jim, I know you love to run on the weekend, but often you over do it and then physically suffer the rest of the week. What are you planning to do to make your week more comfortable as you head into the coming weekend?"

Power Quests have a simple structure that include a beginning, middle and end.

Opening your quest with gentle, descriptive language will be a good beginning to your journey. Try to set the stage for your questions with a brief explanation of what you're looking forward to discovering. As you move along in your discussion you can add probing questions specifically aimed at your target. Remember to bring your quest to an end gracefully. Sum up quickly, and thank your listener for her participation.

> "To listen closely and reply well is the highest perfection we are able to attain in the art of conversation." - Francois de La Rochefoucauld

Yes/No Questions

Be careful of yes/no questions because they can kill a dialogue.

- Would you like to write a book?
- Would you like to change your life?

- Do you like self-introspection?
- Could you imagine living a happier life?
- Can you see yourself a millionaire in five years?

Direct Questions

It might sound obvious to ask questions that get to the point. For clarity, it can be helpful to know a fact in the midst of a conversation. Using the basic *who, what, where, when, why, and how* style of questioning serves this process nicely.

"What would you like to write about?"

Answer: "The sunrays reflecting off the atmospheric, white African sand in the skies over Provence."

- How would you write such a book?
- Where would you start?
- Why would you want to tell this particular story?
- What kind of research would you do?
- How long will it take you to write this book?
- Who do you think would like to read this book?
- When would you write?

Dreaming Questions

Dreaming is a good tactic to help a client see outside her particular mindset. It can be helpful to create new opportunities and see other pathways to the future. Sometimes, I use this type of question to give my clients a safe way to practice making better choices.

- If you wrote a book, what would it be about?
- If you were a flower, what flower would you be?

Sensory Questions

Exploring the senses can be useful, too. If a person is bored with her life, asking about sensations she likes can yield some coachable material.

- How do you feel when you wear red?
- Do you like the temperature to be hot or cool?
- What textures do you like to wear?
- What is your favorite song?
- If you had a theme song, what would it be?

Fill-in-the-Blank Questions

When you want a lot of information from someone, the fill-in-the-blank question can give you what you need. It is a structure that lets the client imagine what they want, who they can be, or anything else you direct with your question. It looks like this:

- If I could be any animal for a day, I'd be a ____ because ____.
- My favorite space in my home is ____ because ____.
- My favorite curse word is ____.
- I know I'm really angry when I ____.
- My favorite scent is ____ because ____.

Bringing in the Heart

"I would say that listening to the other person's emotions may be the most important thing I've learned in twenty years of business." - Heath Herber

One of the reasons I wanted to write this book is because I'm passionate about inspiring other people to create. I do this by quests. My youngest son, who is an expert on my lectures, says I "talk so people can think." He explained that I formulate my discussions with questions that encourage my listeners to probe their own thoughts and participate in the dialogue.

That is what a great coach aims to do. I guess all that mothering was a form of intense coach training after all, because my sons have both turned out to be insightful thinkers, capable of putting their ideas into action. If they were my coached clients, I'd be thrilled at their successes! That's all wonderfully complimentary, and I will pat myself on the back for my hard work, because I believe every parent needs a good thumbs up for their efforts now and then. However, all self-affirming chat aside, what do I do to create this introspection?

I intentionally operate on a simple system. This way I can handle the really complex stuff later.

People do what works for them. So if something isn't going well, understanding what they usually do will reveal the problem. For example, when I talk with some-one who's distressed about a co-worker, I ask specific questions about how that person views working with other people. By asking her to think about what she views as an expected situation, she can usually see what doesn't fit. Then she can create possible solutions to try. It's a lot easier to see the picture, when she paints it herself.

People do what works — think about this like water flowing. Water will always take the easy route, even if it travels through out of the way places. It moves this way in part because of gravity, but also because it's the path of least resistance. Well, now, aren't we human beings over 70 percent water? Yes, we are, and we move through our lives much like the rest of the planet's water — the easiest way possible.

What's the gravity of the situation? What's the path of least resistance? I wonder where my instinctual questions around this person are rooted. One way I ask for introspection is to listen intently for what is actually being said; then, I ponder what works about this. Why this way, instead of that?

It's also a really slick way of telling when someone is lying. My body feels the misalignment when I'm not told the truth. It seems like a ripple disturbing the surface in the pond. I know it in my cells when the calibration of energy around me is disrupted. You probably know this, too. I confess I don't always act on my intuition, and maybe you don't either. When I ask questions and engage another person, I can explore their thinking and discover what is working for them, and that yields what they're up to. Introspective quests can sometimes also be an advantage when we don't heed our intuition and might yield information we can act on for safety sake.

> "The saddest part about being human is not paying attention. Presence is the gift of life." - Stephen Levine

My questing formula is about seeing the whole person — the humble human in the context of what you're asking. It's really easy to plaster our image of what should be all over someone else. However, this truly doesn't work. What I believe is only true for me, and what you believe is your truth, and not mine. While it means more detective work for us, we really benefit from this diversity of belief systems in the long run. Unfortunately, in the heat of the moment, and without a plan for introspective process, we demand answers without contemplating the actions of our quests.

I think this is yet another reason why I love coaching. I love that a specific time and place has been created to focus on one area, thought, action, activity, or creation, and for that specified time, nothing else prevails. Making the place to think, feel, and connect something gives it meaning. Repeating this activity creates a wider connection, as well. It feels wonderful to be seen and heard. We all crave fitting together and need it to thrive. In our fast-paced, got-to-have-it-right-now world, coaching or asking powerful questions offers an antidote to feeling constrained. With coaching, we have a regular place to feel engaged in our quests and fully alive.

When I coach, I love to envision my client in the place she wants to be, but also where she actually is, because this is where we meet. From this spot, we create. From this moment we connect, a new energy begins, and it taps the human heart of the matter. Now we are able to explore together. "What is the spirit with which you attend to your work? Are you happy, stressed, jealous, or tired?" I ask. Coaching affords me the opportunity to sense the human being I'm working with and feel her spirit in the moment, and also in her dreams.

How might you employ this formula if you're a lawyer or doctor? Well, you might ask yourself, "Where is the heart of this client right now? Where do they want to be in one year? How can I help them get there?"

Vulnerability and Humility

Humbleness is another real attribute of being human. It has a secret, too. We need to make space for it. We need to let it enter and exit as it wills, not as we want it to. When you question someone and leave spaces for her thoughtful answers, it gives her the extra room often needed for humility. It's tough to feel humble, because it reveals our vulnerable parts. Nevertheless, these are the very parts of us that make us who we are. Our vulnerability makes us real people, and it's where we touch the deepest part of one another, and this is incredibly powerful.

When you question, respect the holes in other people. They are very important! Often a pause precipitates a humble moment, and sometimes tears obscure it. Let the moment flow, and gently ask your questions with conviction. "How is that diet going?" followed by a pause might turn up some painful truth. "I haven't been able to follow it." Let the pause go on a little longer so the person can feel and hear her own thoughts. Then you can softly ask, "What can I do in this moment to help you lose that extra weight?"

I've been in similar vulnerable conversations where the actual speaking time was about 10 minutes. The feeling time for the coached client was probably closer to a lifetime. The time in minutes may seem like a long time to focus on one question; however, when you think about it, how much time do we actually spend focusing on the truly important questions with another human being?

Our brains never cease to wiz along, chewing on everything we can imagine. When do we make the time for the interconnections we need to thrive?

Coaching or power questing affords opportunities for us to be able to make our lives meaningful and to live out our intended purpose. We can discover how we process our internal thoughts and whether or not they help us achieve what we most desire. Of course, there are numerous other things coaching and quests can do for us through asking great and powerful questions.

Danny, a friend, writer, actor, and also a great coach, shared these responses with me:

Best question I've ever asked:

> "What do you want this to look like? What's your vision of how this should go?"

Best question asked of me:

> "What can you do to be of service?"

His answers illustrate how his value system influences his work. His meaning and purpose comes through in both his questions and the question asked of him.

So where is the heart in your quest? What do you value about what you're questioning? What do you perceive your listener values?

Values

Values are another important key to asking powerful questions, because they help us define what we're dealing with and whether we're on the correct track. Holding a value sets the standard by which we operate. You will be out of whack if you don't follow this standard. The same is true if someone else doesn't follow alongside your value. People are unhappy when their values are violated. Understanding each value - yes, you have many - will help you formulate the best questions.

If I know my client has a value that she always desires to be kind, I can formulate my questions around this fact. Respecting this is her belief gives me an edge from which to launch my quest. This initially works because, for the client, it's easier to feel comfortable when facing facts that, as humans, we're going to be messy and unkind some of the time. I know that she desires to view herself as a kind person; and if she can't, she violates her value system, and if this occurs, we'll be dealing with a crisis. That's usually what happens when we're in crisis — our values have been violated. OK, a line of questioning might sound like:

"So what do you think could happen to set things back on track?"

"How does it feel when you see another reality?"

"Can you imagine another way?"

"Is it time to adjust your value about that?"

Most of us don't see this value stuff coming, so it hits with a thump on the head. I sometimes affectionately refer to it as a "whack attack." When you're whacked, you'll probably want to fix the problem quickly, because it usually means you're stuck until you do. Knowing what the violated value believed is creates the advantage needed to figure out the problem and formulate better questions to aid your power quest.

Let's get back to my kindhearted client. How can I help her see her value might be restated in less problematic terms? I might ask, "Instead of viewing yourself as always kind, how about saying you're kindhearted and human much of the time?"

This would give her the room to screw up and work through it as a human being, rather than rate herself against the perfection she aspires to be. By recognizing and respecting her value, I can help her find a way through her crisis with the inspiration to see something she can create, which by the way, honors one of my values — to inspire others.

When I watch people interact, I notice a wealth of questioning takes place. Everyone internally assesses her own situation. People check on the other person's reactions and measure with their own responses. Mentally asking a barrage of personal inquiries, they sense their way forward. They move like spiders, reaching all around themselves, taking the temperature of multiple possibilities at once. For a human being, the questing process is an enormous act of creativity. It takes a variety of thought, diverse ideas, trial, error, and assimilation of information.

While I like to believe other species can question, I'm not entirely sure if there's scientific proof. Regardless, this ability is what allows us to fully create our world. Questioning and creativity go hand in hand and arguably helps us define our human existence. It takes our spirit and gives us soul. We make ourselves through our questions and define our unique personalities through our power quests.

In this chapter we focused on Strategies:

1. Be clear and concise.
2. Get Responses, not reactions.
3. Know the types of questions.

Chapter Seven Summary Power Questions

What kinds of questions do you normally use?

How will using different types of questions enrich your power quests?

What new ways can you find to bring compassion into your power questions?

What are your core values?

Are there more specific ways you can state your values that include opportunities for you to express your humanity?

How can you use power questions to understand the core values of other people?

What can you do now to prepare for answering the power quest of an emergency?

What are three methods you can use to get the best responses to your questions?

What type of responses are you looking for when you ask your power questions?

How can you redirect your question to get the response you want rather than a quick reaction?

Chapter Eight

Using Creativity & Playfulness — The Tooth Fairy Asked Peter Pan Out on a Date

"The uncreative mind can spot wrong answers, but it takes a very creative mind to spot wrong questions."

- Anthony Jay

Imagine the Tooth Fairy and Peter Pan actually went on that date. Where are they? And what are they doing? No doubt, they're having a ton of fun. I can see them at a mini-golf park. Peter is entrenched in a sword battle with the big clown gate and The Tooth Fairy is giving everyone money. Their matchless quest is in full swing, and they're having a blast along the way. Next, they fly off to the bowling alley, down a few hot dogs and beer, and tie on those crazy shoes. The Tooth Fairy starts down the alley lining up her ball, she runs forward but forgets to let go and tumbles head over heels, wrapped around the ball as it races down the alley. Peter swoops from above to rescue her, but alas, they both end up in the gutter with pins tumbling in on top of them. Undaunted, Peter laughs while he pulls The Tooth Fairy back onto the alley, straightens her wings, takes her hand, and says to her, "Let's go on an African Safari and chase wild tigers."

Quests can be dull or boring, but I recommend you engage your inventiveness and playful side to invite your quest alive. It will wake your sensory output and inspire your questions, and probably enliven the responses you get from others.

Dazed and feeling a bit bruised, The Tooth Fairy pauses for a moment and thinks about what she wants. Peter's impulsiveness left her sore and wondering what might happen while chasing wild tigers. She is used to creating her future, and Peter's carefree attitude raises her concern that she will not end up the way she might want.

In order to create, we must be able to quest. We must tackle all the obstacles of asking questions, receiving informational responses and evaluation before we choose our answers. Questing goes hand in hand with creativity. I often marvel at the way we, as a creating species, have constructed our language. In English the word creation can be rearranged into reaction. What always pops out of my mouth is "Why, how interesting. Was this some alteration in our unconsciousness? Is it a Freudian slip of sorts? Or a mutual spelling of the same activity?" You see, in my way of thinking, they go together.

Here's a little mental wordplay side note. Playing with moving around the letter "c" and you change the spelling of the words. Reaction becomes creation. If you closed your eyes and I spoke the letter "c" you might understand me to say the word "see." "See what?" Might be your initial reaction, but creating a power question sounds like, "What am I seeing?" It's a bit of a brainteaser: With a small shift into a new perspective, you can alter reaction into creation.

Creation can be viewed as a series of reactions. Yet, we think of their independent actions as distinct from one another. We believe either we create or we react to events and information. In truth, we alternate between the two. In order to live what we think, we manipulate our thoughts through questioning; and then, based on the input we discover, we respond in a specific manner. If you think of this process as a chain - a "chain of events" is a good illustration - each link is a step in the process of creation, and every reaction is the twist or turn that differentiates the links.

Communication seems to operate in the same way. Visioning this chatty chain as a "channel of thoughts" might create an appropriate mental picture. We ask questions, which create a series of actions, either physical or in thought; then, we respond in some way. Our act of questioning is like bat radar, always checking where one is in time and space. We talk by arranging sound into thought. We create using questions that alter the elements of our universe. It all flows into a channel, which from point to point can be marked as an event of some significance.

What are the chain of events for this remarkable date? Did The Tooth Fairy and Peter plan them ahead of time, or react to the random spontaneous outcomes of their actions? Without planning your action, you are left reacting to whatever happens. By planning your quests, you give yourself many choices, each with an opportunity to formulate a power question to help find what you're looking for. Without this step, creation remains reaction. Turn your reactions into creations by asking power questions.

As I hope you see by now, in my way of thinking, asking a great question is essential for a good outcome. It doesn't really matter what you're doing, talking with a patient, cross examining a witness, coaching a client, painting a picture, whittling, or writing your book, you will need to master asking clear, carefully crafted questions if you want to get your desired response. You need to be creative, reactive, smart, persistent, and intentional in your questing technique.

Reaction or Creation?

The Tooth Fairy and Peter Pan are creative and playful fairy tale characters. In mythology they both have incredible adventures with a wide variety of outcomes in which their approach determines the way they experience their adventures. Peter Pan is an elusive boy forever stuck in childlike wonder using play to navigate his life adventures. Approaching situations from the opposite end of the spectrum, The Tooth Fairy has many attributed stories about her experiences, some of which are scary, but all of which one could say are based in her attitude, which may not always be considered playful. Her job is one of menial duty, and she uses her creativity to help her get her work done, rather than just having playful fun. When one person's approach is creative, yet serious, and the other's is to just play around, more than a bit of conflict may arise.

Imagining The Tooth Fairy and Peter Pan together on a date, you might conjure up stories of these characters having lots of fun. Remember that the dedicated creative Tooth Fairy paired with fun loving Peter create a different image from a well-functioning, harmonious relationship. To have stability in the relationship, they each will have to make compromises about *always* living with their individual personalities, i.e. The Tooth Fairy's serious attitude, and Peter's playful manner. Sometime in your life you might be paired with someone who is opposite your own personality, and you'll need to find ways to effectively communicate in order to reach your mutual goals. Making use of your creativity and playful expressions can help you achieve asking power questions and improve your communication when dealing with opposing personality types.

What often happens when a person who is serious goes out on a date with someone who likes to poke fun and gets into mischief? What if they marry or become co-workers? Both silliness and seriousness have a purpose;

however, fulfilling that purpose with meaning requires both asking and answering some power questions.

If The Tooth Fairy and Peter Pan decided ahead of time they were going to play for the sheer purpose of having fun, they could create the circumstances where they could cut loose and just fool around for a set period of time. However, if their mutual goal was to enjoy going to the miniature golf park and winning the game, they would have to make a different plan. They could still have fun, but they would need to ask power questions to figure out what strategy they need, and how they might maintain their stamina to play the game in order to win. And, they would need to think about how they would keep their minds focused, so they could actually win the game.

Their power questions would be about what they hoped to experience together. Would they want to merely react to their experiences and accept whatever happens and risk chaos, disappointment, and hurt? Or, would they strive to create their experiences and challenge each other by planning their actions for their date?

"Creativity is the sudden cessation of stupidity."
- Edwin Land

Creativity Plays a Role in Everything We Do

Creativity. The universe simply would not exist without it. When you view your world from a creative vantage, nothing is impossible, implausible, or unreal. Everything happens! Our minds explode with vortices of imagination. Innovation is the active interaction of our thoughts and ideas.

Our capacity for creativity is astonishing. We don't just order a "#5 with cheese." We create our order by the way we ask for it. We visualize and taste it. We feel our hands holding that cheeseburger, and we smell it for minutes and for miles before we eat. We interrogate our schedule for when we can arrange that drive to our favorite fast food joint or the walk to the fridge. We look at our watches and plan. All of which take multiple, sequential questions.

"What time will I eat?"

"What would taste great today?"

"How can I make time to go to Sloppy Sues for my favorite sandwich?"

"Will I have it with those allspice pickles?"

"Maybe I'll try the brown butter mustard?"

"If I leave early, could I stop by Jensen's and pick up a Carmel coffee?"

"If the sun stays out, will I have the time to eat in the rose garden?"

We quest to others and respond to other's quests right from birth. A newborn cries for its parents to respond. With practice those cries are refined into specific demands. There is the "I'm hungry" cry, the "Change me" cry, the "Touch me" cry, or the "Let me scream to exercise my lungs" cry. Parents begin to understand their child's cries, because they're actually primal questions.

When a baby cries, and her mother responds, "Are you hungry?" "Do you need your diaper changed?" or "Do you need a cuddle?" they're off on a powerfully creative quest.

We communicate with our senses and our facial expressions as much as with our words, just as we have from the beginning of our lives.

Risk, Emotion, Sensory Exploration, and Illustration

How can you use creativity in formulating your questions? Take risks, free emotions, indulge in sensory exploration, and incorporate varied illustrations to deepen your creative queries.

When you share your risks, you reveal a bit of your humanness. Remember, we're all vulnerable, and it's this part of our character where we can honestly be present with one another. Taking a risk within your quest will also help you experience new, powerful creative paths along the way. Exploring different opportunities can provide a rich atmosphere for your responses to flourish. Try something new the next time you ask someone a question, and watch the creativity it brings to your adventure.

> M. A. Rosanoff: "Mr. Edison, please tell me what laboratory rules you want me to observe." Edison: "There ain't no rules around here. We're trying to accomplish somep'n!" - Thomas Edison

Don't be afraid to let your feelings show as you ask questions or when you get a response. Feelings are natural communication and, as creative beings, our feelings can be like a paintbrush, adding magical strokes to everything we investigate.

Notice the different sensory opportunities that can exist within your quest. Are there any missing senses you can add? If you find ways to ask your questions from the perspective of sight, sound, touch, taste, and smell, you will add many creative enjoyable elements to your process of discovery. How might you ask someone for directions involving sound? Or how about questioning to share memories through smell?

Make sure you find different illustrations to explain your questions. This will ensure you receive the best responses possible. Creating differing platforms gives you and your listeners many avenues to probe for answers. It also helps the journey be more interesting and lots of fun!

A couple of reminders to create great and powerful quests:

Never Be Perfect

The Japanese made an art of this practice called Wabi Sabi. I love it! It means that everything is in its place for a reason and you don't always need to manage things in perfect order. The Amish made their quilts with one square in colors that was a tone off from the rest, so they didn't offend God with their perfection. Baltimore quilts often had one square that didn't seem to fit the design for the same reason. You aren't supposed to be any more perfect than you are already. When you screw up, and you definitely will, apologize and ask something like, "Well, isn't it refreshing to be human after all?"

Silence is a Jewel

With all the noise in your life these days, silence can be a jolt: especially when you are face to face with someone. Don't let it tap your anxiety. Learn instead to observe what is happening around you.

I'm so amazed at the amount of noise at different times of the day. I notice how I play with the volume control on my TV remote. During the morning it seems people and commercials are louder than the midafternoon. My volume control lands near 15 in the morning and down a bit to 12 a little later in the day. However, by dinner time everyone seems to be screaming at each other. The volume goes to 26 to hear the news, and then on mute, because the commercials are broadcasted at 32 or higher. Late at night I can hear the sound at a volume of nine. What's up with all the sound level tinkering on the broadcast end? Why do they need to play with the volume to get our attention? It's no wonder we get anxious dealing with a moment of silent connection. We're not used to it!

Use your quiet time to learn about connections without words. A deep breath will inspire those around you to do the same. Sensing your feet on the ground underneath you can be a welcome sensation. Without lots of noise, it's much easier to figure out where you are in time and space. We are in a far more natural state when we remove unnecessary noise. Theme park executives have mastered the skill of tweaking rides to alter our sensibilities so we experience the greatest fun, but when you're on a power quest, you have to be the master of your own senses. You have to know how to make it fun for yourself.

Sometimes, as practice, I watch TV without the sound and sharpen my awareness of gestures and body language. It's another way to play with a power quest to imagine the storyline without sound. I did this recently on an airplane. I was watching a movie I hadn't yet seen, and I tried to figure out what it was about by watching in silence. Later I asked someone who actually saw the movie what the actual story was about. I pegged the storyline, silently!

Here's a tip: If you feel you must speak, but can't think of anything to say, be quiet, or your foot may protrude from your mouth. You might want to trust me on this one because, remember — I have lots of...err, experience.

Simply put, there is nothing wrong with silence. In fact, I happen to require it more and more these days, and I can imagine you do, too. So when silence feels uncomfortable, remember you don't have to fill it. Just sigh sweetly, smile, and receive the quietude as a gift by asking yourself, silently, "Isn't the quiet space peaceful?"

"Great is the human who has not lost his childlike heart." - Mencius (Meng-Tse), 4th century BCE

Play

Play is often used in the creative process, but play by itself is not the creative process. I think this point is often confused by many people. Often I hear, "Oh, you're an artist. It must be so much fun to play all of the time!" The truth is, I don't play as often as I wish, because if I played most of my time, the serious work of my creating would not be done. The thinking, planning, analyzing, hypothesizing, work setup, as well as the practice and the mundane repetitive effort of showing up every day, even when I'd rather be off playing, must be done to be a creative soul and actually produce work. Play is a rambling, freeform, spontaneous effort. Creating is an intentionally planned and artfully executed activity.

It's important to realize that using your creativity requires many tools, one of which is play. When you ask your power questions, it's important to be a bit playful from time to time, because that allows for spontaneous inspiration that can bring new thought into your quest. The adventurous attitude of play can breathe life into your power questions.

I've explained a little about why, as an expert on creativity, I wrote this book. Even so, as an expert on play, why would I write this book about asking power questions?

I call myself "The Play Wizard" because I help my clients discover the magical benefits of playing. I help them learn to play as adults. By teaching them why they must play, we explore the avenues of their spectacular growth and connection to life.

You help define your meaning and purpose through the ways in which you play. Did you know that it is a natural state of your being to play? Your brain cannot work without playing. More than that, you cannot learn and grow or evolve, unless you're playing - amazing, huh?

"Too much of our work amounts to the drudgery of arranging means toward ends, mechanically placing the right foot in front of the left and the left in front of the right, moving down narrow corridors toward narrow goals. Play widens the halls. Work will always be with us, and many works are worthy. But the worthiest works of all often reflect an artful creativity that looks more like play than work." - James Ogilvy

We're bombarded with the message that when you grow up, you do not play — unless you can earn, justify, or find the time and money for it. I bet you know what I'm saying. "Oh, grow up will you!" translated means: "Stop playing around!" However, you cannot — you will not grow without play!

I'm not a scientist, and this is just my take on what I've read from the recent research. Nevertheless, I do see fantastic results when I apply my playability methods in my workshops and coaching sessions. People love to play. When we're playing we are at our most basic and real selves as wholesome human beings. We were designed to play. Our survival and happiness depend to a very great degree on our ability to play.

"One who asks a question is a fool for five minutes; one who does not ask a question remains a fool forever." - Chinese proverb

OK, so as The Play Wizard, what I know is that play underpins everything we do, how we think, and how we communicate! We actually are built to access our world through play. Our brains are wired to play. It is the method we function within, and is the basis for how we think and act. Like I said, I'm not a scientist; however, I do know from experience what I'm talking about. When I help my clients bring play back into their lifestyles, good things happen. And I mean really, really wonderful things.

I hear this question all the time: "How can I play before my work is done?" So I developed several programs for helping adults manage to bring more playtime back into their lives. They're precisely designed to tackle the stuff we feel prevents us from being more playful. You'll find more information about what I do to help folks play on my website: www.meetyourmuse.com. Whether you're interested in a workshop or not, please do invite play into your daily routine.

> "We all operate in two contrasting modes, which might be called open and closed. The open mode is more relaxed, more receptive, more exploratory, more democratic, more playful and more humorous. The closed mode is the tighter, more rigid, more hierarchical, more tunnel visional. Most people unfortunately spend most of their time in the closed mode. Not that the closed mode cannot be helpful. If you are leaping a ravine, the moment of takeoff is a bad time for considering alternative strategies. When you charge the enemy machinegun post, don't waste energy trying to see the funny side of it. Do it in the "closed" mode. But the moment the action is over, try to return to the "open" mode — to open your mind again to all the feedback from your action that enables us to tell whether the action has been successful, or whether further action is need to improve on what we have done. In other words, we must return to the open mode, because in that mode we are the most aware, most receptive, most creative, and therefore at our most intelligent." - John Cleese

Once again, I ask this great power question: Why would a play expert write a book on asking powerful questions? I wrote this book because I see a direct link between play and questing. For me, they go together like strawberries and cream. There are a number of ways we play. All of them use some kind of a quest. Some types of play rely on it. In my work, I recognize how important questing is for us to be able to play.

Play is important to our human existence because it creates new neural pathways. Your personality has a specific way it likes to learn, and you need to play for this learning to develop. So, how does one incorporate play into her daily life and work?

For me, I professionally teach workshops about play and bring playfulness into my coaching practice; and, when I make art, it's a playful celebration. I see a good power quest in the same vein as I view a great game of play.

Imagine Fred, who likes to tell stories, but he needs to know about his characters before he can spin a good yarn. So he power quests to learn about them. Both his questioning and his play unite.

Mark likes to play sports. He wants to learn to play tennis. He needs to formulate and ask the best questions to figure out the optimal strategy he'll use to play.

Ginny loves to paint. She will need to ask clear, specific questions about her technique, the tools, and paints she'll use as she creates. This back and forth between questing and playing will result in a finished canvas.

If you're in your forties or fifties, you're probably as far away as you'll get from the childlike wonder of play with which you started your current life adventure. I'm basing this on life expectancies, of course. You may already be really playful. If not you'll need to work to get it back, but the process can be lots of fun!

> "The best way to have a good idea is to have a lot of ideas." - Dr. Linus Pauling

I'm writing a more in-depth book about the benefits of play and creativity where I'll share fun techniques about the magic of creative play. For now, let me say that play is important in order for you to create; and, creativity connects your quests. When you're formulating a question, you're playing around with your thoughts and the words that illustrate them. When you play tennis, the very act of playing the game involves the same techniques of asking a powerful question. You need to understand the rules, your ability, and that of your opponent's, as well as figure out your strategy to win.

Since I know about the habitual ways we play, I can relate to different personality types and how they approach the game of questing. If you like to move your body or play sports, you're going to approach your questing as though you're training for a big game, event, or match. It will be a bit different for you if you like to tell stories. You'll be inclined to approach your quest as if it's a great novel unfolding in chapters, where every character holds intrinsic meaning for you, and offers details for your quest. We play in numerous ways and each of us has our preferred style for a quest. If you participate in my Play Wizardly workshops, you'll come to more fully understand how you can use playful styles in your own quests.

"One advantage of talking to yourself is that you know at least somebody's listening." - Franklin P. Jones

Playing is one of the human being's highly specialized techniques for assimilating and understanding the world. We gather our information through play. We imagine our future through play and we connect to one another through play. We can't create without it. And, I dare say, we can't communicate without play. Therefore, we won't be able to question our experience without play.

I like to play. I rarely stop playing. I let it invade most everything I do, and I tease others, adding a bit of play into our activities together. Having a playful attitude means that you will be asking a few questions here and there. I was one of those kids who repeatedly asked, "Why?" And, I always, always asked, "Why not?" in response to every "because..." answer I was given. I wasn't being precocious. I just had, and still have, an instinct for knowing there might be more to the story, and now I understand a specific way to get to it — power questing!

I'll even let you in on a little secret, but you'll have to read my next book to find out how it works for you. Every one of those playful habits, and the people who used them, that I mentioned earlier has a specific kind of quest at heart. What could this mean for you? It means you have a basic style in which you play and go on a quest! And I know what it is, but you'll have to wait for my book or take one of my workshops to find out how you can use it. Okay, enough teasing, but consider this my invitation to come along and play with me.

> "A person might be able to play without being creative, but he sure can't be creative without playing." - Kurt Hanks and Jay Parry

I challenge you to be a kid again and play the "Why/Why not?" game, challenging everything you hear for one hour. You might need to do this with someone who is a good companion, because adults tend to get irritated by it quickly. Your boss or doctor might not catch on that you're playing with them! I guarantee you'll have fun and probably discover some new information. Sometimes, even seeing something you already know in a different way can be magically inspirational.

The Hope Is

Bring playfulness into your quest using these simple suggestions:

- Have Fun
- Observe Others
- Play Together

- Explore

- Imagine

- Smile

Have Fun — Make your quest an action game. I don't mean to turn it into a ridiculous sport; rather, create some fun aspects to how you think, formulate, and ask your questions. Make up some game rules. You can set parameters such as a time-frame about when you'll ask your questions and when you want your responses. Alternatively, create other rules such as asking all the brown-eyed people first. There really is a method to playing from a game stance because it will create for you the opportunity of a new perspective from which to view your quest.

Observe Others — Listen and take note of questions asked by others and their responses. What works? How do they begin talking? When do they insert questions? How well do they listen? Do they repeat what they heard before they go on? What tips can you take away and put into your own quest?

Play Together — Find playmates. Surround yourself with play-minded people. Folks that enjoy having a good time will also have a good time joining your quest. Another benefit of playing with others is that they can further your quest in their own circles and help you gather interesting responses to your questions. You can learn much from how they go about it, too.

Explore — Try new things. Experiment by changing the style of the question you ask. Shifting from a "why" question to a "how" question can yield some helpful information you might not have otherwise received.

You could also ask someone who is new to you. Often we get complacent and stuck in our own happy ruts. Shake things up a bit and talk with a stranger.

Imagine — Find ways to elicit stories from others by asking in a story like fashion. "Imagine if you wake up tomorrow and everything is different. How would you begin to explore?"

Smile — You'll be surprised at what wearing a smile, when you question, will do for your quest. When we smile, we create chemicals that flood our entire bodies with really good things. We benefit from these nice chemicals, sort of like an energy drink. Imagine how this natural elixir will infuse your questions with energy!

Flashing your smile at someone else can cause them to experience their own natural, positive energy. In addition, you communicate so much with a genuine smile that you'll be establishing your values and building great foundations in your relationship.

> "Without the playing with fantasy no creative work has ever yet come to birth. The debt we owe to the play of imagination is incalculable." - Carl Jung

In this chapter we touched on Strategy:

1. Be creative and playful.

Chapter Eight Summary Power Questions

How can you make silent moments powerfully enrich your quests?

How many ways can you reframe your power questions to make them more playful?

What kinds of creative elements can you add to your power quests?

How does the noise level around you affect your exchange of information? What might make it more powerful?

In what ways might your playfulness or creativity inhibit your power questing?

How can you use the idea of story or metaphor to enhance your power questions?

How many different ways do you play?

What is the most creative aspect of your power quests?

What fairytale bests represents the way you've been questing?

If you could go on a quest with any fairytale character, who would it be? Why?

Chapter Nine

How to Ask Power Questions — The Billy Goats are Gruff

"There is no such thing as a worthless conversation, provided you know what to listen for. And questions are the breath of life for a conversation."

- James Nathan Miller

In the tale of the Three Billy Goats Gruff, the ugly troll beneath the bridge is fooled by the first two goats. The troll demands to eat whoever walks across his bridge. But, he's not fully paying attention to the sound each goat makes as it crosses the bridge above him. The first goat is small and tells the troll to wait for the next goat who is fatter. The second one says to wait for the next who is tastier. When the last and biggest goat comes across, the troll says he'll now be eating him, but the goat easily and gruffly butts him out of the way.

If you're not careful and don't pay attention, you, your questions, and your quest may well get butted out of action, too. In this chapter I'm going to share a few points about how you can make the most of your questioning skills.

Tone and Timber

The sound and pattern of your voice matter to your quest — a lot! Learn to manage your voice for the best impact you can make. Sometimes, you need to speak in a loud, clear voice. Other times a whisper will do. Think about what fits the result you want from your conversation, and then speak your carefully crafted questions in the tone that serves the dialogue.

The sounds we hear actually kick off chemicals that cascade throughout our bodies. Individually, we have our own reaction to these chemicals. To ask the best question, you need to pay attention to the sounds you make, in order to get the kinds of responses you want.

If you have a high-pitched, squeaky voice, work to change it to a lower sound. Take a deep breath between questions. Soften your gaze, and relax your shoulders. Speak slower than normal. Speaking in a voice that mimics a siren will elicit a primal fear reaction from your listener. You're shooting for a response, not a reaction. If you naturally speak in a high-pitched voice, you can retrain your voice by learning a new speech pattern just like actors do.

Tip one: If you're a woman, and you're having a hard time communicating with men, listen to your voice. Is it high and squeaky? How about whiny and tearful? If so, you might as well be pouring hot oil in their ears. The sound of this kind of speech is like a high-pitched jet engine. It's actually physically painful for some men to hear. Think about this: does a siren hurt your ears?

Tip two: If you're a man, and women resist listening to you, check your voice level. Are you talking loud? Women may interpret this as being scolded. Do you like someone yelling at you?

Speed is also important. If you speak too slowly, in our ever speeding-up, fast-paced lives, you might not get heard. People are actually hearing faster these days, and their patience is shortening! Try not to make it painfully slow to listen, and perk up your pace if needed.

Talking too fast is also very irritating. It seems to raise the heart rate of those around you. It certainly does mine. Try to slow down so your listener isn't ready to plug their ears from your lightning sonic boom!

My Grandfather used to tell a few family stories over and over. I knew them by heart and, as much as I loved the connection, when he told them, listening to his very—slow—pace—was—difficult. My grandmother had a hard time hearing me, because as a kid I talked very fast. Pay close attention to the reactions you're getting from your audience. Are they tracking with you? Do they show signs of interest in what you're saying to them? Are their eyes just glazed over? Are they squinting at you? Are they wincing as if they hurt somewhere? Are they interrupting you and asking "What?" repeatedly? If these don't fit the response you want, change your tune.

Like many people, coaches work and communicate by phone and the Internet. How can you tell if your client is alert and in tune with your quest? This is a very tough and important question if you work with people in these mediums. As professionals, we all have our methods, and we know we need to be aware of making sure they're working for our clients. If we're in doubt, and it isn't as easy as it sounds, we must ask important questions and check things out.

Email can be easily misunderstood. Any emotion may become one dimensional and has nowhere to land. Asking questions needs to be carefully thought through and read with a literal deciphering of the words you use. If you don't hear a response, you better check it out and make sure you were understood. It takes a while to get the knowledge about how both parties communicate and find the rhythm that works best for both of you.

My favorite story illustrating this came from a good friend of mine who taught deaf children. I asked her why they didn't often eat with the rest of the school. And she replied: "The kids only understand the flat translation, not the emotional or humorous descriptions. They take the words literally, and they paint the picture of meaning in their minds. The last time we went to the cafeteria, the menu read 'Hot dogs, open-faced turkey sandwiches, and black-eyed peas.' After reading it, the kids imagined horrible images and they all ran back to their room terrified." Be careful writing email quests!

Questing by phone is, for many coaches, the most common way we serve our clients. It has its own quirks, but for the most part, I think human beings have now evolved to talk on the telephone with its many variations of technology. My point is that we use phones all the time, and we're used to doing so, which makes phone coaching or questing this way comfortable for many.

One of the most important skills you need to develop when you communicate by phone is to completely use your ears. What you hear may be more important than what you actually say. Becoming comfortable with a phone pause is essential for anyone deep in a quest. You want your listener to think and feel her way through what you just asked, and since you can't see her, you'll need to trust the pause is working. Of course, if the pause gets very long, you might want to check and make sure she didn't drift off to sleep! Holding the pause is a strong skill every great power quester needs to master.

Attitude

The attitude you have when you ask your questions will also have an impact on the response you get. When you ask power questions, if you're not mentally available, you'll do mediocre work with your audience. How you fashion your own attitude is important to the outcome of your query. Short questing sessions are great because they can be very powerful. It's much easier for people to keep their attitude positively focused in thirty minutes, in contrast to an hour.

Body Language

You can tell a lot about a person by watching her body response, and she can tell lots about you by watching yours. You can also pay attention to your posture as you talk. I spend lots of time on the telephone talking with clients, and I make sure where I am and what I'm doing relates in a positive way to my client. Sometimes, I pace with them, other times I sit calmly and pay attention to my breathing.

Wearing a smile will radiate throughout your voice and infuse your voice and attitude with your energy. It's a simple thing to do. When you answer your phone, do you frown with suspicion or light up and smile? Your caller will know!

While it's usually helpful to match your emotion to your listener, you'll need to tread carefully in situations where they're negatively excited or agitated. I wade into the coaching sessions gently. The skill I'm talking about is where you emotionally reach your client and subtly move them to a different place, where you can actually coach or quest with them. This is a developed skillset and not one to try if you're unable to manage angry people, or if you are fearful of and shy away from conflict. There's nothing wrong with being honest about this.

Conflict is uncomfortable, and you need to be able to fully hold your own emotions out of the equation to help your client or power quest with someone in a difficult place. If you're meeting for your session in person and cannot manage the client's anger, be prepared to shut down the conversation and set another time to talk — making it clear that you cannot coach or interact when the person is this angry. Anger comes up, and it is a part of power questing and certainly coaching, but for the most part, careful thought and manner can move everyone into positive territory.

When you capture your listener's emotion, you can test whether they're ready to move forward, out of they're anger. If they aren't, you'll need to be patient and ask questions to focus on where they are; and, if necessary, boldly move to another time to chat.

You bring energy to your quests and the people you question, and it's very important you take responsibility for this exchange. If you're having a bad day, it will show. If you're communicating via phone or Internet, it's important to remember your attitude will impart energy into your conversation. There are other energy contributors of course, and you'll need to pay attention to them, as well. I do a whole body check before my sessions so I know where my energy levels are. Sometimes, I know a client is high energy, and I'll need to stay on top of my own vigor to stay with them in a session. You can use whatever tools, methods, or training you have to meet this requirement of asking powerful questions.

In this chapter we touched on elements relating to many Strategies:

1. Listen carefully without letting your emotions interfere.

2. Be calm and open. Breathe.

3. Hold your own character and characterizations back.

4. Don't confuse.

5. Be clear and concise.

6. Stay focused.

7. Be patient.

8. Be creative and playful.

9. Use the right voice.

10. Use HALOS

Chapter Nine Summary Power Questions

How does you voice help or hinder your power questing?

In what ways do you find your attitude influences your listener? In person? On the phone? In an email?

When you quest in person, how can you use your body language to get the response you want?

How can you perceive the body language of your listener when you're speaking by phone?

What are the ways you can handle a power quest that gets into unmanageable territory?

How might using the technique of HALOS help you to actually ask the most powerful questions?

Chapter Ten

Dialogue Snatchers —
How Cinderella Got Her Prince

"Many 'active listening' seminars are, in actuality, little more than a shallow theatrical exercise in appearing like you're paying attention to another person. The requirements: Lean forward, make eye contact, nod, grunt, or murmur to demonstrate you're awake and paying attention, and paraphrase something back every 30 seconds or so. As one executive I know wryly observed, many inhabitants of the local zoo could be trained to go through these motions, minus the paraphrasing."

- Robert K. Cooper

Oh, those wicked stepsisters! And the evil stepmother's orchestrating and mischievous meddling to thwart Cinderella's happy ending! If it weren't for the Fairy Godmother creating a glass slipper, Cinderella would still be sweeping out the cinders.

I'm not going to lie to you. There will be more than a few rascals trying to hijack your commanding mission. You are going to need a glass slipper and maybe some of your own magic to stay on your quest. Your goal is to create and maintain a dialogue so you can ask really great and powerful questions.

Dialogue stealers take control of a conversation and prevent it from growing. If you are speaking to such a hijacker, you'll need to regain control of the conversation. As a coach, I use those mighty powerful questions to stall a chitchat captor in her tracks. Here are a few of my favorite examples of dialogue snatchers.

The Passive Speaker

Passive speakers may be shy, calculating, introverted, uninterested, annoyed, angry, or in any number of emotional states underneath the surface of their speech. They're also capable of stealing the dialogue, because they can quickly shift the focus, which can thwart or divert your agenda. They're usually thinking elsewhere, and are certainly agile enough to masterfully command what they want. They often like word games and take the role of letting you guess. Learn to recognize this style for the game it is. This is not a dialogue.

Listen in:

"Hi Betty, what's been going on this week?"

"Oh, nothing special."

"Tell me about the un-special things going on."

"M-m, you know I did the same old stuff."

"No, I'm not sure I do know what the same old stuff is."

"The same stuff we talked about before."

"Can you be more specific about which stuff we discussed?"

"You know, the stuff about my job and my boyfriend, and my mom."

This kind of questing will go on until you inject a directed question:

"Betty, what would you like to talk about?"

"Betty, how would you like to use this coaching session?"

"Betty, how can I most serve you this week?"

In fact, once you peg this type of dialogue snatcher, you probably want to make it a habit to start off your time together with a directed question and stick with it.

Angry Talk

We all get pissed off now and then. Anger is our human pressure valve, and we need it to work well. We don't need it to prevent us from living our dreams. When you power quest with an angry person, you'll need to respectfully acknowledge the anger and treat it honorably. This is also a good coaching model everyone can apply in some way to their relationships. Respect and anger do go together. However, we weren't taught this as kids. Therefore, many of us adults just avoid angry situations at all cost.

Think about this: if you could be assured that it's okay for you to get angry now and then, and you were cared for in such a way that your anger was honored as a valid and important part of you, wouldn't you let your anger out more easily? For me, this notion diffuses my fear of my anger. I create the space to be angry and feel the benefits; yes, there are great benefits to honoring my anger - being honest with my feelings, respecting the lessons learned, and discovering yet another mystical level of my soul, to name a few. After all, emotions teach us who we are and where we are in time and space. Stop denying anger exists, and address it respectfully.

Listen in:

"Hey Gary, what would you like to talk about this week?"

"I'm really mad this week."

"What are you mad about, Gary?"

"Someone broke into my car and stole my laptop. I had my book draft on it."

"Wow, that's really awful. How can we process through your anger about this today?"

Tip: If the person talking to you elevates her voice, duck!

We naturally raise the sound of our voice and speak in a more raised tone than is normal when we're agitated. (Remember the siren voice).The higher it goes, the more we blow! If you sense this happening in your client, see what you can do about it. Diffuse it, if you feel safe doing so, and work with the material you discover about it as soon as possible. Until the air is cleared, you won't get much further in your quest with that person.

Baby Talk

If you speak in a way that sounds like a baby, will you be taken seriously? Would you take a baby seriously? I hear adult women who speak to people in a childish voice, and I wonder what they want. I personally don't like to be talked to in baby talk, because I'm not a baby. I find this communication approach disrespectful. I usually make it a habit to talk to this type of client using bigger adult words and breathe in ways that invite her to lower her voice. It's also interesting to observe that this type of person often has difficulty knowing what she really wants to do with her life, and exploring that journey can be noted in the change of voice and speech to a more adult sound.

Up-ending Sentences

I also get annoyed with that nasty habit of up-ending sentences. This is a habit in which speakers raise the tone of their words at the end of everything they say. They confuse the difference in voice pitch between making statements with asking questions. I get the sense that the speaker is trying to land somewhere, and the whole time they're talking, they're circling the airport. If I want to fly with you, I'll buy a ticket. When I have clients flip into this talk, I intentionally state my questions by lowering the pitch of my words at the end of my statements. This can infuse clients with a bit of confidence to fearlessly speak with conviction. It may just be my way of adding balance, but it does seem to have a positive effect. We are after all part simian — it's my professional aberration of "monkey see, monkey do." It is important to speak with authority when we make our statements so our questions stand out as powerful queries.

Vulgar Talk

I don't believe in censorship. I do believe in speaking so others can listen to you. The difference between censorship and being heard is about making your own choices. I guess it depends on how you look at it. I prefer to make my own choices, feel the privilege of my freedom, and own the consequences of what I say.

Vulgarity definitely has its place in our speech. It is a powerful spot and needs to be cared for so it is ready to use for our own protection. What do I mean by this? Swearing lets people know something about us. When I swear, my friends and family understand I'm challenged by a boundary I hold dear. They respect me, and therefore my rules, and they have no doubt what I mean when I boldly say "shit!" Sometimes, I swear in a humorous or teasing way. Yes, there is a loving, funny, gentler mode in which to say, "Fuck you!" Like when my bluff is called. But, for the most part, when people swear all the time, it's unclear what they're trying to say.

Going on a quest with these clients will be illuminating, because they haven't heard the underlying eloquence of their own words. Your job will be to both craft questions they will understand from their current speech and gently nudge them to find other words that tell more.

Listen in:

"Hi Joe. What's been going on this week?"

"I had a shitty week. It was fucking awful, again."

"What was awful?"

"That God damn boss of mine is such a shit head."

"What happened Joe? Something up with your boss?"

"Yeah he's up to the same old crap. He just doesn't fucking get it."

"What doesn't he get Joe?"

"That asshole screwed up my hours again. He's such a fucking pig!"

"So, your hours are screwed up. What does that mean?"

"That fucking asshole has wrecked my vacation!"

"Joe, I'm confused. How do your vacation and screwed up hours fit together?"

"That fucking..."

"Joe, I get that your boss is a jerk, but I'm confused about your hours and vacation. Can you explain that to me?"

"Yeah, I was working overtime to save money for a little vacation, and now that jerk of a boss screwed me out of it!"

"I can understand how disappointing that is for you, Joe. I know you really need a break from work and your boss."

"Yeah, I do. That asshole..."

"Joe, I wonder if there is another way you could reach your goal of a vacation without depending on your jerky boss?"

"Like what?"

At this point I have plenty of opportunities to explore with my client. Furthermore, he has begun to discover options through my using different words. By changing the vulgar description of Joe's boss into a "jerk", I demonstrated both that he is still unsupportive to Joe but perhaps perceived to be less provoking, always ready to upset Joe.

Changing the words also serves to diffuse the situation, but you first have to acknowledge vulgarity serves a purpose for your client. Hold the space for them, acknowledging the powerful feelings, and substitute easier to hear words whenever you can.

The reverse situation may also present itself in your work. You may have a client who really needs to express some dampened feelings, and vulgarity will serve them well. They can be a whole lot of fun to help release through questing!

Listen in:

"Hi June, how are you?"

"Oh I'm fine."

"Tell me what's been going on this week."

"Well my supervisor said some things to me that were upsetting, but I'm sure she didn't mean them."

"How were you upset? What were you feeling?"

"I felt really angry at first, but I know she was careless."

"What did you do with your anger?"

"Oh nothing, I probably shouldn't have gotten so upset."

"Why not?"

"Well, I never do."

"Uh-huh, what do you do with the energy of the anger?"

"What do you mean?"

"Where does it go? Does it leak out, steam off, fly over... I know we've talked many times before about your anger at this supervisor and the mean things she says to you. Wouldn't you like to tell her something back?"

"Well I guess so, but that wouldn't be very nice."

"What if you said it to me first? Then you could decide if you wanted to say it to her later."

"OK, what do I say?"

"Swear at her."

"What?"

"Really let her have it. Give back to her all her meanness."

"SHIT! FUCK!..."

Have fun and show your client it's OK to be vulgar in the circumstances that need a little more boost.

Victim Talk

I have grown out of my own victim mentality and now have a profound annoyance about it in others. It only seems to serve the victims, but from personal experience, I don't believe it truly serves them at all. In the process of questing, victimhood is a real dialogue snatcher. When you craft a line of questions for victim talkers, you'll need to be very aware of how they twist and turn your words to create a self-inflicted, terrorizing situation. Their life experience has conditioned them to believe the world is always out to get them. They may not know they have a choice to think in a more positive manner about how they can interact with the world.

This is a sad state of being, but it can be dealt a dose of positivity with careful direction and attention to your chosen words. First, don't believe their situation is completely real. It may be the reality in their own mind, but it is rarely the truth of their existence. My grandmother made a big deal that the family didn't care enough for her because someone decided to serve a ham one holiday, which she believed she couldn't eat. Her doctor had told her to cut back on salt. She took every opportunity to drive the stakes in that we didn't love her. Needless to say, it wasn't a pleasant dinner. After the meal, she jumped up to clear the table, I followed only to see her in the kitchen clawing at the ham, ripping off chunks and eating them like a frenzied wolf. Nothing serious happened to her health. Her relationships with the family were another matter to repair. The point is, we can get ourselves into belief systems that don't serve us or the ones around us.

Asking questions about "what will happen if..." will usually yield clear cut results you can work with to identify where the person is stuck. Be gentle and take your time. It can be like walking in a minefield. Doctors and lawyers must deal with this sort of thing just like coaches do. Sometimes, it takes a team effort to right the balance of these individuals. For example: Suzie worked with her Creativity Coach to help identify the whole picture she was living within, and this helped her develop a plan to move beyond and into her dreams. Her coach pointed out she needed to check some physical complaints out with her doctors. Her doctors fixed some of Suzie's physical problems and suggested a lifestyle change, which required a lawyer's services to shore up her legal situation. It took an entire team to help her change her life from one of victimhood to a freer life where she felt healthy and happy.

Something has usually happened to these people that left them unsure about trust. So when you question them, work to ensure they are safe and feel safe talking with you about such things. Stop them when they get going into a long diatribe about everything that's wrong. You only need to hear enough to determine the pattern of their thinking. Turn negative, defeating comments they state around.

"So I hear you need a vacation, where would you like to go?"

"Oh, I'd love to go to someplace warm with a beach."

"What would you do there?"

"I'd sit on the beach and read all day."

"That sounds great. What needs to happen for you to take this trip?"

"Oh, I could never go on a trip like that."

"Why not?"

"With my back! I couldn't carry my suitcase."

"What if you found a way to move your suitcase that didn't hurt your back? Could you start packing?"

"Oh no, even packing would be too painful."

"Could you find someone to help you pack?"

"Well maybe..., but..."

"If we found a way to remove all the obstacles so you could manage this trip, would you still want to go?"

"I don't know..."

And this is the response you'll need to work with over and over, within different situations, until this client decides they are ready to try something different. Hopefully, with the gradual chipping away of obstacles, from your carefully crafted questions, your client will make lots of little changes, which will all add up to a big measurable shift.

Sometimes, clients just aren't ready to work. They like the idea of changing and living a happier life, but the work is too much. If this happens, face it, your client has closed off any other possibilities but her own misery, and yours if you don't look out! Victim talkers crave company in their pity pit. You'll either be blamed that you just don't understand, or she'll use the experience to prove to you she was right all along. Her life sucks — move on politely to someone you can serve.

Internal Gremlins

Yes, every trained coach knows about these creatures. There are many varieties of internal gremlins, and they are usually the silent part of your client, at least at first. Beware! They have the nasty habit of jumping out and messing things up. Asking your clients questions about what they say to themselves will usually expose these gremlins for what they are. I've also noticed these clients almost always speak in phrases rather than complete sentences, because they're trying to keep themselves from completing the thought, which might actually lead to productive action. Helping your client flush out these pests and restate thoughts in complete sentences removes the gremlin's secret power. And you have initiated a forward moving power quest with your client.

Dialogue snatchers are habits we all have and need to deal with often. They can interrupt a great power quest. However, they can be managed with a little thought and planning.

In this chapter we covered Strategy:

1. Dialogue snatchers.

Chapter Ten Summary Power Questions

What common dialogue snatchers are you able to identify?

What are the personal strengths you have to deal with angry or vulgar people?

How can you use your compassion to manage dialogue snatching and not let it derail your power quest?

How do you know your power quest is about to be snatched by your listener's dialogue?

What does a snatched dialogue tell you about your listener?

What can you do if you realize you've just snatched the dialogue?

Chapter Eleven

Don't be a Lemming - Lemmings Don't Quest or Look in Mirrors

"I only wish I could find an institute that teaches people how to listen. Business people need to listen at least as much as they need to talk. Too many people fail to realize that real communication goes in both directions."

- Lee Iacocca

My husband likes to play 21 questions with me. It goes like this:

"What's that?"

"Something I need."

"For what?"

"Work."

"Where does it go?"

"Somewhere."

"Where?"

"I'll move it later."

"What does it do?"

"Something."

"What?"

"Why do you want to know?"

"I'm curious, it's on the kitchen counter. What is it?"

"It's something I need for a project."

"What Project?"

"A thing for work."

"Which project?"

"Sumpterville."

"What does it do?"

"What do you care?"

"Just tell me what it does."

"It's a thing for a radio antenna. Why?"

"Oh, I thought I could use it to skewer potatoes."

"No! You can't! Why would you do that?"

OK, I admit it, I cheat. By the end, I get him so flummoxed he asks the questions. If you have one of these types in your life, you know how frustrating it can be to find out what's going on. It's also an interesting display of a simple quest.

Remember, we all have a little part of us that is pure lemming. Yes, that little rodent part of us would rather follow blithely along, not having to work hard or think about anything beyond our own thoughts. The bug-eyed and long wispy whiskered piece of us would like to not figure anything out. Be honest, aren't there moments when someone is asking you something but you'd like to not be bothered thinking about what was just spoken to you? Do you lose patience with the 21 questions style of chat? When you want a hamburger, you just want a hamburger, right?

Let's listen in:

"Can I take your order?"

"Uh, I want a hamburger."

"Would you like a single, double, or triple patty?"

"Um, a single hamburger."

"Quarter pound, one third pound, or half pound?"

"Quarter."

"Would you like cheese?"

"Uh, sure."

"Cheddar, American, Swiss, or provolone?"

"Oh, cheddar I guess."

"Would you like any ketchup?"

"Yes."

"Mustard?"

"No."

"Pickles?"

"Yes."

"Tomatoes and lettuce?"

"Tomatoes, no lettuce."

"Onions?"

"No onions."

"Would you like mushrooms for an additional 25 cents?"

"No mushrooms. I just want a hamburger."

"Would you like mayo?"

"Yes, just a little."

"Would you like to make it a basket?"

"OK."

"Fries, onion rings, or cheese curds?"

"Fries, I guess."

"Curly, French, or seasoned?"

"Regular."

"Which regular: Curly, French, or seasoned?"

"French."

"Did you want a drink with your hamburger?"

"Sure, a cola."

"Which kind..."

You get the picture, because we often get into this kind of discourse. So, here's the truth of the matter: Who, but you, knows what kind of hamburger you want?

The most important thing I want for you to hold in your mind here is that if you can't ask a clear question, what makes you think someone else can understand what you're looking for, much less answer it?

Try asking this way:

> "Can I get a quarter pound hamburger basket with cheddar cheese, tomatoes, pickles, and mayo; regular French fries and a coke?"

When you're in a situation where you're not hearing the answers you want, listen to yourself. Getting to what you want will require you to speak clearly, and not assume the other person understands you. What exactly are you saying? Hear your own words. Are you leading the conversation with smarmy comments, assuming the other person will understand your crafty wit and acquiesce to your brilliance? Why wouldn't you receive a curtsy? After all, you figured it out, you genius! Wake up. Your sarcastic, cunning wit is lost on the lemming masses. Why should they care what you want anyway?

Mirror, mirror on the wall. Who's the power questioner?

So to ask power questions, you have to hear yourself and your requests, and then convince the other person to want to tell you what she knows. You need to understand and know in very clear terms what you want, and you do this, in part, by listening carefully to what you are asking. How can someone else learn what you're asking, if you don't clearly understand it?

> "The trouble with the world is that the stupid are so confident while the intelligent are full of doubt."- Bertrand Russell

Knowing and applying are the tenets of higher education, and cognitive thought is worthless without application. That's why I believe cutting out school recess is criminal! The same goes for work breaks and vacations. We need the time to apply our knowledge, or we get stupid — very stupid! Lack of playtime is detrimental to our intelligence. We need to play to put our ideas into action so we can experience the consequence of our own thoughts. We need experience to help us learn and actually make wisdom.

Mentally play around a bit with past experiences where you had verbal altercations or disagreements. Did you know which of your words could actually get what you truly wanted? If you did, why didn't you ask using those words? Sometimes, the truth is we just want to feel we're right, and not bother with the process of getting what we want. However, think about what's most important for you here, being thought of as an intelligent person — perhaps a genius among lemmings - or getting what you need? I could be wrong, but I've never heard of a lemming named Einstein. In your quest, you can be smug or self-deprecating. You can also learn to speak so others can listen. You can ask the powerful question and find your answer. You don't have to follow the Pied Piper.

Don't beat yourself up if your questing needs help. You can be very smart but this whole concept of power questing might be new for you. Take your time and explore your options to learn.

> "There are people who, instead of listening to what is being said to them, are already listening to what they are going to say themselves." - Albert Guinon

Mirroring

Mirroring is a human phenomenon backed with scientific research. We copy one another all the time. In fact, we also see this in nature among the flora and fauna that decorate the planet. Every universal pattern has a component of reflection.

A human baby responds with a like reaction to its mother. Lovers engage each other, responding to the gentle touch of their invitations. Friends collect familiar answers from one another, and strangers test the safety of interaction through posing questions and judging answers. The action of questioning enables us to navigate our existence.

Mirroring is a form of visual questioning. With looks and physical expressions, we formulate our ideas into questions and watch for the answers to appear in response. We also do this when we converse with each other.

Here's a response from a graphic designer in regard to creating a theme:

What's the best question you've ever asked?

"What was your inspiration?"

What's the best question asked of you?

"How can we make it better?"

Both parties in this conversation played off each other's question, reflecting elements of the characters back into the dialogue.

As a painter, I capture what I sense and see internally then project it upon my canvas. It hangs as a mirror for people to gaze into and ponder what they feel. I view my paintings as creating mirrors that beg questions of my audiences.

The evil queen consulted her mirror for truthful intro-spection. You can ask yours to give you powerful questions.

"There are no dumb questions—only dumb answers."
- Marshall Loeb

Actuality or Reality

In our minds, we each live in our own self-created world. This becomes our reality. It works until we forget that it is only ours to see and know. Other people can't know about our reality unless we tell them. They also have their own to manage. This is cause for confusion if one doesn't clarify what specific world the parties will convene within.

Most of the time, we step to the edges of our own reality and then glance around at other people and the circum-stance that they appear to us to be within. When we question, it's important to recognize that this is the natural state of mind in which we all exist. It takes an effort to step beyond our edges and meet another person in a new space. Asking a great power question can create this brand new reality.

To do this, you'll need to move from your reality into actuality, the state of what actually is true, rather than what you believe to be true. Just admitting you have your ideas about what to believe and I have mine will be the first step, because it acknowledges there is something more than what you or I alone think. Accepting we all come out to the world from within our own diverse thought processes, allows us the freedom to ask ques-tions that reveal the really great stuff of human beings and the universe we live within.

Excuses: Only, If, But, When, or Then

Listen intently for these little power punched phrases, because they will annihilate the spirit. Help your client's rephrase their words into more self-appreciating and productive language whenever possible.

The cues for excuses are ever present, though sometimes subtle to the uninitiated ear. Listen to the speech of those you encounter, and then listen to your own. Plug in the words you hear following "If": "If I had more money, time, was prettier, better educated, was loved better, happier…"

How about what you hear after "Only": "I can't because I only…, If you only understood me better, if only… Someday!"

Then there are those awfully negative "BUTs": "I could write a book about my life, too, but I don't have the time…, but I don't have the luxury…, but my book's not interesting…, but who would want to read it…, but no one cares."

"When"? "Then"! "When pigs fly, then I can…?" Who's being fooled?

Pay attention to your own speech, and see where you are living in a time warp.

"If" — This simple word signals a fantasy. It may be just a dream, and unrealistic. Encourage your client to complete her statement and notice where it disconnects to her actuality. Then reroute it with a power question. "What will you do to make that idea an actual opportunity for yourself?"

"Only" — Translated, this word means I can't because… Learn why your client feels this way. Challenge her to know why she's consciously chosen this position. "How will you accept that decision and move forward?"

"But" — I'm not able... I don't have whatever, yet... This word always negates something that came before it was stated. It foretells fantasy butting in with pretense, stalling the flow of truth. When a client uses the word "but", I look for a hidden agenda and/or a negative attitude. It's important to listen carefully and ask questions before I react to these folks' commentary. Ask your client, "What are you erasing?" "What aren't you telling me?"

"When"/"Then" — These two words may signal your client is dreaming without a plan of conviction. Encourage them to not put off what they want until their future yields nothing. "What would it take for you to make that dream something you can honestly engage with in actual time, within six months?"

"Should" — We use this word as proof of our judgment and to empower our untruths. The word speaks of fanciful forecasts. Hearing "Because you should," demands that someone wants you to fulfill her fantasy. I truly despise the word "should".

This one word has caused more disease, discontent, unhappiness, and frustration. It has affected everyone, including children and old folks. The poor and rich, the wise and stupid do not escape its reach.

We are given the nourishing banquet of linguistic choice, yet we feel completely starved by this one word. It has stimulated, provoked, afflicted, and motivated the most unholy actions in all of us. It is the impetus of the greatest carnage one can do to another soul. It has one of the most innocent appearances, and subtly fills in for the "good intentions" we desire. With lightning speed, it initiates reaction and leaves — indiscriminately — permanent damage everywhere. Our use of it is careless, though its target is precise. It is the perfect weapon, still drilling the kill long after its initial deployment.

If it were up to me, I'd erase this word from the dictionary and cause us all to explore better communication. Using the word is easy, cheap, and quick — the lazy soul's shortcut. We think it says so much, believing we actually own and originate its power, but it's the devil's spawn spewed from un-love. As long as we use it, we remain unconscious and judgmentally disconnected from humanity. Challenge yourself to use a better word. You will not ask powerful questions using the word — "should!"

Now for a really spellbinding word!

"And" — "And" is a magic word that tells a truth.

Authentic folks use the word "and" to express both sides of an issue. It helps them speak from the truthful standpoint of full inclusion. "And" has real power. I use it intentionally when I speak. It opens from one heart leading to another. "And" connects, rather than polarizes, offering choice. Using the word "and" in your power questions is a real asset.

Catch-up or Ketchup

Stop procrastinating and make meaningful connections. Remember to take the time you need to be in person with friends and family. A powerful quest is one that includes a majority of live interactions so all of your being can be involved. Remember, ketchup is a condiment you put on meatloaf; catch-up is an important activity that builds good relationships.

Why don't lemmings quest? Because they're four-legged, furry creatures and they're not supposed to ask questions. Don't just blindly follow. You're not a lemming — Ask powerful questions!

In this chapter we focused on Strategies:

1. Hold you own character and characterizations back.

2. Recognize differences.

3. Be a navigator.

4. Get responses, not reactions.

Chapter Eleven Summary Power Questions

How would mirroring your listener's response help your power quest?

What kind of words help you achieve your desired power quest outcome?

Do you have any specific speech habits that help or hinder your power quests? What might those be?

How can you manage the habit of playing 21 questions and get to the point of your power quest?

Other than "should", how many other words can you use to formulate a great power question?

How can you make sure that when you speak to someone else you are both operating from the same reality?

Chapter Twelve

Powerful Coached Quests — The Emperor and the Gingerbread Man

"We do not grow by knowing all of the answers, but rather by living with the questions."

- Max De Pree

How can you ask your questions so others can hear you? By now I hope you've realized that achieving a powerful quest requires more than a few skillsets. Though simple in form, the skillset employed will need some preliminary thought to engage your listener.

As a professional creativity coach, I've needed to master these skills. Throughout this book I've shared many of my techniques so you can apply them in your own power quests.

There are a few more key skills every great coach must have in order to give true value while serving their clients. They are not mutually exclusive from one another, but work in tandem, building a powerful foundation for the coaching process. You may not be a professional coach, but you can wear your — HALOS - the last of my 17 Strategies and well worth rereading, because if you get this right, you're well along on your power quest.

Hearing

Articulation

Listening

Observation

Sifting

Hearing is essential for a good conversation. Coaches hear everything: the tone of your voice, sound cues from your environment and your verbal reactions to them, all background noise, the expression of your audible energy levels as they rise and fall. They hear what is actually spoken, or avoided. They pay attention to the things you may not be aware are influencing you.

Articulation is a masterful skill, and one that good coaches understand well. They know when to speak and how to phrase the words for the most impact. They are capable of telling you they truly care about your welfare and are able to create a good outcome for your coaching experience. They hear your words and know how to use them to ask the great questions you want to find answers to.

Listening is usually thought to be a simple, passive act. But, we coaches know better. True listening is an active action that involves the whole being. It takes undivided attention and commitment to be a good listener. Coaches listen for the cues that let them know where you are in your journey.

Observation is mostly about perception. What a good coach knows about you, they gain from perceiving your expressions, as well as reactions and responses to questions and ensuing conversations. From this, they know what to explore to get you to your desired goals.

Sifting is a subtle skill that helps the client make decisions. Coaches challenge you to move through their questions. The coach uses the quest to act like a sieve, carefully sorting through your information for the golden opportunities. Examining your facts and fiction will transform your challenges into successes.

If you're a coach, a manager, or anyone having trouble with any of these skills, ask yourself why you're questing? You would benefit from hiring a coach yourself and exploring why you're on your quest and what you hope to accomplish.

The best coaches I know are people who have a genuine desire to help, the patience to carry out the process, the training and skillsets to craft a great coaching plan, the experience to know how the work gets done, and the wisdom to understand that each client has unique possibilities to reach her goals.

People don't believe you care until they know you care. When you quest, how are you asking about them that shows you care? You have to illustrate this with your questions. As a coach, I sort out lots of my client's information and ask lots of questions. I use the underlying formula of: "Why are you?"

This question can be used in other professions or personally, too; even if you don't ask it directly. Be a perceptive detective and learn all you can about the person you're talking with. How do they see their world? What do they believe in? What gets them out of bed and into their day?

Just think about why others are the way they appear? - "Why is that little old lady walking like a penguin?" "Why is that man talking so loud on his cell phone?" "Why is that young woman angry at the kids she's with?" "Why can't that business man look you in the eye?" "Why did the driver of that car cut in front of you?"

> "Effective questioning brings insight, which fuels curiosity, which cultivates wisdom." - Chip Bell

Awakening your own sensors will help you ask power questions and open up productive dialogues. When you question, it's important to remember that you can be a mirror, reflecting your listener. Having awareness of your client will help you see the blocks and holes in their beliefs and desires. You can then help them align themselves with becoming the being of their choice.

Awakening the Senses

- If ____ (your job, vacation, relationship, boss), were an animal what would it be?
- What did that smell like?
- What color is your favorite day?
- What's your favorite feeling?
- What color is your favorite night?
- How does your body tell you that's true?
- What color is your favorite piece of clothing?

The Emperor's quest ended with him naked and the Gingerbread Man's ran wild. What kind of quest do you want to have?

What's your story?

The sum of who you are right now is what's important.

We tweet in bursts, little notations of who, what, where, when, why, and sometimes how we are. Using just a few characters to say our peace, we need to be seen, to be heard, and to ask our questions.

Whether you like this or not, you are captured eternally in the digital moment - frozen infamously as you are right now. It's a new social communication with its own lingo and meaning. And questing is still at the core of it all.

Questioning is the major mechanism humans use to navigate, communicate, postulate, and celebrate. It may always have been this way, but now, more than ever before, we need to be very conscious of this fact.

Pauses

Remember the silent pauses are the main tool of a great coach. Don't fill in the blanks for your client. Let her flounder. Let her feel the consequence of her own making. She's paying you for this service. What can you do with a pause? Be still and observe. Listen to what is not being said. Let your client stumble around while you hold her safe in this space of wonder.

Dreaming

As a coach, I help people live their dreams. In order to do this, I need to explore their dreams with them. Coaches use a variety of questions to discover this information. Here are some samples:

- What's the next level?
- Where do you want to be next week with regard to this topic?
- What do you hope to gain from ___?
- When it's over, what do you want to remember?
- Who do you want to be with when you live this dream?

Explorations

I also help people explore their opportunities for learning and success. This line of questioning is a lot like offering encouragement to a child riding a bike for the first time. You want to help them explore all the reasons why they can't, by helping them to see all the reasons why they can.

- How will you explore this idea?
- Who will you ask for help?
- Why do you feel this is the project for you?
- Where will you focus first?

- How will you know? How will you measure your accomplishments?

- What do you specifically want to know?

Pointed Questions

These types of quests are usually fast and direct. Practicality comes to mind here because this quick method is clearly hunting for something quite specific.

- When will you make your payment?

- How much will you be paying?

- What time is your appointment?

- Where is your car?

- Why do you need a blue shirt?

- Who do you want to speak with?

Goals

Setting goals for your quest isn't any different than any other blueprint. You have something specific you want to know, and you create a plan to figure out the answers about what you want to know.

If I want to bake a special chocolate raspberry cake, I'll need to lay out some specific questions to help me bake.

- Why do I want to bake this chocolate raspberry cake? This is one of the most important questions to ask in order to set power questing goals. Understanding your desire and motivation will yield the crux of what you want. It's a great first question.

- What recipe will I use? This will help me formulate a list of possibilities and opens the opportunity to discover how other people approached this task.

- Where will I find the best recipes from which to choose? I'll need to explore the vast resources available and the different places I'll find them.

- Who can I ask for help? This will give me a list of people to query. And I'll learn other great questions about this process from them.

- When will I want to bake this cake? Now I'll need to assemble a timeline upon which my questions will float.

- How will I bake the cake? This question helps me to plan specific parameters around my quest. How will I know I succeeded? If your answer to the first question was, "because I want to see it on my favorite glass cake stand," how are you going to mark that moment? Will you have a party and note what your friends say? Or maybe you'll need to plan on snapping a photo so you'll have a record of baking that delicious chocolate raspberry cake.

There are infinite ways to plan a great power quest. How will you plan yours? What methods will you use? Set a goal or two to reach for your quest. What do you really want to achieve? Who do you most want to question? When do you want to reach answers that will serve you? What do you hope to gain from your questions? What approach will you use?

Exit Questions

An exit question serves several purposes. It signals it's time to sum up, and can define how to move on. During interviews, there is a volley of questions and answers, all hopefully leading to some good discussions in the middle. When it's over, it's time to create an ending to that quest. In a coaching session, that may be just before the session is up. A good coach doesn't leave her client hanging, rather she ends when the energy is high and focused.

Listen in:

"Well Tom, you've done some amazing work today! How would you like to build on this next time?"

"Tom, you worked hard to uncover these discoveries today. How would you like to move forward?"

"We need to end in a few minutes. What about your next steps would you like to discuss?

"How can I hold the essence of you until we talk next?"

Voice

Become aware of the tone of your voice. Know the emotion of it and how it changes what you're asking. This can be quite useful or heavily judgmental. Actors practice this skill until they get really good at it, because their job depends on it. So do many other professionals. What you're saying inside your head does show up in your voice.

Can you listen to yourself? Really hear what you're saying in that small, internal voice? Smiles are heard loud and clear! So plaster one on from the inside out when you ask your clients questions, and you'll appreciate the results.

"There is no such thing as a worthless conversation, provided you know what to listen for. And questions are the breath of life for a conversation." - James Nathan Miller

Well there you have it. Now you know what a powerful question is and how to ask it. You've learned my 17 Strategies and the creative coaching skillsets to put them into action. You've discovered the many benefits of powerful questing, and hopefully you desire to go forward with power questions.

Whipiddy-spit! I've waved my magic wand…

Now it's time for you to begin your quest and *ask power questions*! Let me know how your power quest unfolds.

Email me: sandy@meetyourmuse.com.

Chapter Twelve Summary Power Questions:

What will your tale be?

Where will it begin?

Does it have an ending?

Who are the characters, and what will they do?

What do you want?

What steps will you need to take to get this?

Where will you begin, and when will you start your quest?

APPENDIX

Useful Power Questions for Specific Fields

> "A prudent question is one half of wisdom."
>
> - Francis Bacon

Introductory Questions

Adult Children

Actors and Comedians

Acupuncturists, Chiropractors and other Care Professionals

Artists

Automotive Technician

Bankers

Bosses

Cab Drivers

Cancer Survivors

Caregivers

Coaches

Creative Minds

Customer Service

Dancers

Digital Artists

Doctors (Medical)

Elders

Employees

Fiber Artists

Financial Advisors
Friends
General Service Providers
Graphic Designers
Hair Stylists and Specialists
Hearing Impaired and ADD
Lawyers to Clients
Lawyers
Massage Therapists
Men
Mentors
Musicians
Painters
Patients
Physical Trainers
Quilters
Sculptors
Store Clerks
Students
Teachers
Teenagers
Terminally Ill
Weavers
Women
Writers

Introductory Questions

These little gems will almost always evoke some kind of interesting response from your audience. Play with them and be inventive with the way you ask them.

- If you were a flower, what kind of flower would you be?

- What stage of your life cycle would you be in?

- I know I'm playing when ____.

- I have always wanted to ____.

- The world is a happier place when I ____.

- The secret I'd most like to share is ____.

- The secret I always feel I need to hold close is ____. Why? How do I hold it close?

- My friends would be shocked if I told them I ____. Why?

- The rock, gem, or crystal that best represents me now is ____. Why?

- What are you hungry for?

- My favorite month of the year is ____.

- If I ranked the four seasons, number three would be ____. Why?

- When I hear a child's laughter, I ____.

- My passions are ____.

Adult Kids

If you have adult children, you've probably learned a whole new relationship develops as they come to live their lives as grownups. What this brings to you is that you need a whole new way to interact with them. No longer little kids (although, at times, they may still act like it in your presence), they are now responsible for their own actions. You don't have to pick up after them or tell them what to do. In fact, telling them is now a thing of the past, unless you are speaking fondly about the past. At one time or another, all of my 17 Strategies will be helpful to you when asking them power questions, but perhaps my most important tip is to pay attention to your emotional tone and facial gestures.

It seems to me that to have a great power quest with your kids, a good goal will be to recognize you are now a special friend with privileges, and that those privileges come with the enormous responsibility that you maintain yourself as an adult, too. Sometimes, that's pretty loaded stuff to wield in a family conversation, so think about what you're going to ask and maybe even try it out on a good friend first, just to get some feedback that your emotional tone is well placed.

Remember, you are still the parent, so you need to guide by modeling and at the same time be an adult about it. Here's some powerful questions to stimulate an adult conversation. Steer clear of yes/no answers, if you want to engage your kids, and recognize their amazement when you talk as if you now know they really do know something about life — and you value learning about it from them.

- How do you define your role in the family now?
- How can I treat you respectfully?

- When can we get together to chat? (They will probably want to know: chat about what?)
- What can I do to help?
- How can I support you with that project?
- Would you like me to ask someone else for advice on your behalf?
- How would you like our relationship to grow?
- Where do you want to be in five years?
- Considering the family or your career, how do you see yourself living in ten years?
- What is your plan for your personal future?
- What's on your bucket list?
- What are your plans to achieve your bucket list items?
- What is your financial plan?
- When is the best time for me to call you?
- What are your favorite childhood memories?
- What family heirlooms would you like to have one day?
- There are some important things I need to tell you soon, what's the best way for us to connect? (You may need to be more specific about your time frame.)
- Would you be willing to help me with _____ this weekend? (Be specific about what you need them to do. This isn't any different from asking a repair person for services. You may even consider payment in some form.)

- Hi! How are you today? (Don't forget to just listen!)

Actors and Comedians

Actors and comedians can be vulnerable, and they are also somewhat resilient people. Keen observers, they study people all the time. They look to discover the little inadequacies that define us. They are really good at stepping in and out of themselves, and because of this skill, they're marvelous questers. Here's a list of questions you might ask them to engage in a conversation about what they love to do. But be aware they're often experts at my 17 Strategies, and they may turn the power questions back on you!

- How do you prepare for auditions?
- What do you do in order to get in character?
- Where do you rehearse?
- Where do you find inspiration?
- What do you do to stay fit (mentally, physically, spiritually) in order to perform?
- What's your favorite role?
- What role would you love to play?
- How do you celebrate your achievements?
- What makes you laugh?
- What makes you sad?
- What is your favorite audience?
- How will you handle criticism?
- What do you look for in a director?
- What will you need to do to prepare for that role of a lifetime?

Acupuncturists, Chiropractors, and Naturopathic Care Professionals

In my experience acupuncturists, chiropractors, and naturopaths trained in their areas of expertise because they truly want to help other people improve or maintain a healthy lifestyle. They've also been creative in their choice to do so by stepping out of the medical mainstream. While many of these nonmainstream professionals are not aware of this aspect of their personality, you can use your creativity to enrich your power quests with them because they are often open to creative influences. I've found them to be committed to their style of care and usually have quite a passion for implementing it. All of my 17 Strategies can be helpful at one time or another in dealing with these types of folks, but I've included a few power questions to get you started in a good dialogue quest.

- Where did you train, and why did you choose that school?

- Can you teach me how this style of care works?

- Where do you find your best inspiration?

- How long will the treatment process take?

- What can I expect during and after treatments?

- How did you choose this profession?

- How long did you train to do this?

- What can I do to participate in my treatment?

- How do you define what you do?

- How do you perceive we can be partners in my healthcare?

- How can I communicate with you outside an appointment?

- Can you point me to qualified resources about my health needs?

- If you were in my body, what would you do?

Artists

These are my kindred folk! I speak from the heart when I say that we do like to talk about our art; however, we always take a risk when we speak about it, and, sometimes, we don't know what to say, how to say it, or are afraid to say anything. Be gentle with us and avoid making pronouncements such as, "My grandchild can do that, why do you do it?" Instead, ask really nonjudgmental, probing questions, and you'll find out some really insightful and interesting facts. Also, remember the 17 Strategies work best when you combine them, and artists will usually love the variety of powerful questions you can bring to the quest. All artists are treasure hunters, so give them cues for powerful visual amulets to open up new creative doors. This helps them think about their creativity in a new light and gives them inspiration. Here are a few powerful questions to get you started.

- Where do you find your best daily inspiration?
- How do you capture your ideas?
- How do you engage in your art daily?
- What is your technique?
- How would you want to market your art?
- Where do you want to show your art?
- How do you define being an artist?
- Do you want to make a living off your art?
- How might you make a living off your art?
- How will you stay fit for the challenge of being an artist?
- What will you do to maintain your creativity throughout life?

- What meaning have you discovered through making your art?

- Do you make art for the sake of it, or do you want to share it with the world in some way?

- What do you do with the leftover art or practice pieces?

- How do you sort out all of your fantastic ideas? (We artists do need lots of compliments!)

- What do you think the purpose will be of leaving an artistic legacy?

- How do you see art, creativity, and the playfulness of making art helps humankind evolve?

- Who is your favorite artist? Why?

- How many times have you practiced this idea before you painted, sculpted, or sketched this piece?

Auto Mechanics

We all need auto mechanics and their skills. It may be hard to find a knowledgeable and honest mechanic, so when you have them, it's important to keep them. They may look grungy, but remember, their work is dirty, and they're just struggling hard to make a day's labor. They're passionate and have invested a lot of time and money in their craft. Did you know they have to own their own tools, and those tools cost many thousands of dollars? So does a proper education in auto mechanics, as well as ongoing industry certifications they must master just to work on your car. Consider all the thousands of inter-working parts on your vehicle; now note all the systems: fuel, multiple electrical systems, computers, power train, hydraulic, brake, and numerous safety structures. And don't forget all those creature comforts we insist upon, each one another component in the massive motor vehicle system: heat, air conditioning, lights, sound, power seats, back-up cameras, and DVD players. This work takes real brains, brawn, and commitment.

We ritualize and worship our vehicles. Don't believe me? How anxious are you when you have to leave your car at the shop? We spend an enormous amount of time in our cars, and they've become our sanctuary. We view our cars as our private space, and we commune with it every time we climb in, adjust the mirror, and turn the key. It is an extension of our very selves, and we need someone capably talented to maintain it for us.

Mechanics have gotten the reputation of being gruff, rough around the edges, not very bright bulbs to begin with, and other derogatory labels. Did you know there are multiple computers within your car? That your car has around 15 to 20 miles of wires and a more complex electrical system than your home or laptop? That it has over eight toxic, hazardous chemicals and substances that each need specific and careful handling? That your airbag is an explosive devise like a small bomb that can explode in the mechanic's face, too? That when you bring your car to the shop, the engine is over 200 degrees on a cold day and needs to cool down so they can safely have a look? A good auto mechanic needs to know about and handle all of this information to keep your car working. Use all 17 Strategies when power questing with them.

They deserve to be communicated with in a respectful manner and held in high regard for their skillsets to maintain your private temple. Treat them well, and they'll do a respectful job maintaining your private space. Here's some mechanic inspired and appreciated tips: Always wash and clean out your car before it goes to the shop. No one wants to work in your filth. Don't be afraid to tip, or in some way gift, your mechanic for a job well done, and be patient, because good work takes time. You may be paying a high price for the work, but the mechanic doesn't get all that money, and they hustle putting in their sweat and brains to fix your car's problem. Above all else, be honest with what happened, what you did or didn't do yourself, how much time you truly have to wait, and how much money you can afford to spend right now. They have clear cut ways of figuring out if your story is false, so don't play any games with them, and they won't with you. Don't forget to say thank you.

The best question my mechanic ever asked:

How much money do you want to put toward repairing your car?

The best questions asked of my mechanic:

How did you figure this problem out? How long did you train to learn all of this?

- How is your day going?
- How long will it take?

- Can I wait?

- How much will it cost?

- Can it be done cheaper with other parts?

- Will you let me know if you find anything else wrong before you fix it, so I can budget the cost?

- What is the most pressing problem that needs to be fixed right now?

- Can I leave my car and pick it up later?

- What do you recommend about ____?

- I realize you are very busy. Can I pay you to look at this problem, or answer my question right away, or shall I schedule an appointment?

- My concern is that it is safe to drive right now, or while I wait for my appointment. Is there an interim amount of work I can pay for now to make sure?

- What are some signs/symptoms I need to pay attention to so I know if I need to pull over and call for a tow?

- What can I do to properly maintain my vehicle?

- I'd like to drive this car for another three years or 50,000 miles. In your professional opinion is this worth fixing?

- In the long run, is it going to be cost effective to make the repairs with used or rebuilt parts?

Bankers

Finance folks are interesting to me because they work and communicate in a narrowly focused area. Answers to my questions often sound black or white when I quest with them. I've found to get real power questions going, I need to utilize the Strategies of asking, using very few yes/no questions. However all of the 17 Strategies can be helpful at one or another time when questing with them.

I confess, I can't help playing with these linear thinkers so I do ask creative questions now and then to get to know them as real people and not just bean counters. Have some fun with them for yourself, too, especially if you're working with your money. Here's a tip: most of them do like a good joke. I can't explain this, but it seems true for me.

- How is your day going?
- What is the policy about __?
- Who is responsible today?
- Who is the branch manager?
- How can I contact that department directly?
- Do you ever get tired of counting money?
- What happens if you make a mistake?
- How do you assess the fees I've been charged?
- How much money do you think will be enough to reach my goals?
- What specific financial planning would you recommend for me to do X by Z?
- What do you do for fun?

- What's the biggest counterfeit bill you've collected?
- Can I have my change in real gold?
- What are your hobbies?
- How big is your piggy bank? What color is it?
- Do you have a hammer to whack my piggy bank?
- Read any good books lately?
- What's your favorite kind of story? What did you like about it?

Bosses

Ahem, we need to deal with our bosses. Hopefully you have reasonable and inspiring bosses. All 17 Strategies will be a boon for you to work out power quests with them. Be patient and observe your full communications carefully. They can teach you lots about yourself without uttering a word, as well as when you engage with them in conversations. I can offer this tip: your relationship with your boss is, and will always be, a power (authority) stilted dynamic. Don't expect it to be anything else, like a friendship, because at the end of the day, you still work for her (hopefully). Remember you are being paid to be professional.

- What can I do to improve my skills? (You might want to be more specific at times. What can I do to improve my skills for this project?)

- Will you show me how to do it? When can we schedule a time?

- What other resources can you recommend?

- How long do I have to complete the project?

- Will you give me a review? When?

- Can you suggest a mentor? Who?

- What can I do better right now?

- Can you show me another way to be efficient at this task?

- How do you define your position or role with me?

- When can I have a raise? How much money can I expect?

- What role do you want me to take in this project?

- What is my deadline to complete X?

- What resources do you recommend I use for this part of the project?

- Will I receive more money or other compensation for adding these (be specific) items to my workload? What will it be?

- Can I negotiate for a different responsibility within this project?

- What is your preferred way for me to bring complaints to your attention?

- What is your process for resolving conflicts?

- What is your policy around dress codes, handling personal matters at work, or other rules for employees? Is this written in a manual? When/where can I get a copy?

Cab Drivers

I know lots of people who don't talk to their cab drivers. They think it isn't appropriate for an assortment of reasons. When they sit in the back of the cab, a wall goes up between the seats. Not me! I ask all sorts of questions of cabdrivers. I love their unique perspectives on life and the environment we're traveling through. When I'm in a new city, I look forward to my cab rides because these people know where the heck I am. They know the places to be, and how to get there - something I don't know in a new place. They are people with a special window breaching the world I want to explore. Every one of the 17 Strategies will be helpful while you power quest with them.

- Could you tell me where to find the best restaurant for sushi?

- What's the best time to leave to beat the rush?

- Do you have any tips for getting to the museum in the morning rush hour?

- Where's the best place to hail a cab outside Macy's on 7th Avenue?

- What's the cheapest fair to the airport at seven o'clock on Sunday morning?

- Can I call you for a ride? Do you have a card?

- What do you like best about this city?

- What do you recommend tourists see?

- What's the weather really like here?

- When does it usually rain?

- What do you like to do for fun?

- What brought/keeps you here?

- What's special about this place compared to where you came from?

- Why is this city a good place for art, music, sports?

- Where's the best place to watch local people?

- Why do you stay here?

- What unusual experiences have you had while driving your cab?

- Would you recommend walking in this neighborhood at night?

Cancer Survivors

These are people living on the edge of the here and now. They grope through denial of their disease to define a new life. Sometimes, it brings about major lifestyle changes, and other times, it just changes the pace at which life is lived. But, remember for them and their loved ones, there is always something scary off in the distance that sooner or later they must face all over again. Most survivors go through rechecks, tests, and follow-ups that only awaken all the numbing fear and anxiety usually inwardly blocked by denial. This is sensitive stuff, and I know the 17 Strategies will help you navigate your powerful quests with them.

- How are you doing today?

- How is your health right now?

- What are you planning for yourself today?

- What have you learned from your experiences?

- What do you want to focus on today?

- What do you want to accomplish by the end of today?

- Do you want to talk about your illness?

- When would be a good time for you to get together to ___? (Be specific about what you want to do.)

- Do you feel like having some fun this weekend? Can we plan something?

- What can I do to be supportive?

- Are you okay with me bringing up your health situation?

- What can I do to help you keep up the hard, important work of maintaining your health?

- How's your family doing with all of this? Is there anything I can do for them?

Caregivers

This group of people needs lots of mirroring, support, and understanding. They're usually lost in giving a loved one care, all while they are suffering, too. It's so much harder to watch someone suffer than to deal with it directly. Caregivers need to be seen as the person they are underneath all the treatment and concern for the patient. They're actually a patient suffering, too. Their lives will forever be altered, and they're completely helpless and don't receive any care from the patient's care process. They're often responsible for managing the patient's care and left to fend for their own care. In the midst of all the expectation placed on them, you can do a lot for them by asking powerful questions that help them survive and possibly thrive.

The best question asked of a caregiver:

"How has all of this affected you?"

The best question a caregiver asked:

"What do you need me to do for you right now?"

- How are you doing with all of this?
- What do you need right now?
- What's the hardest thing for you right now?
- What would make it easier for you?
- If you could take a break, what would you like to do?
- Is there any support you need?
- How can I be there for you?
- What would you like to talk about?
- What would you like to do together today?

- Would you like to share what your life used to be like?

- What do you miss about life before the illness?

- What help do you need to make plans for yourself?

- Would you like to take some time away from caregiving? When and how can I help you with that?

- When did you eat last?

- Are you sleeping?

- When was the last time you took time for yourself?

- What chores do you need help with? Can I do some of them for you this week?

- Do you have enough support, or maybe too much of one kind?

- Can I help you manage the support you have?

- If tomorrow were the way you wished, what would it be like for you?

Coaches

Sometimes, a really great coach is hard to find. However, you will know them by the questions they ask you. They focus on you, reflect your stated goals, and tap into the mystical way you want to reach them. Their words will thump you on the chest and see into your hidden parts. They will have the ability to fully embrace you, stopping your thoughts and altering your patterns, so you can realign your thinking with the pathways of your dreams. A good coach will ask you questions that may sound like:

- How big a step do you want to take this week?

- What do you most want to accomplish today?

- Where is your focus today?

- What do you want to focus on today?

- Is your story make-believe? Can you live it?

- How far can you leap during the next month?

- How can you live your dream now?

- What breathes life in your dream on a daily basis?

- What's stopping you from doing what you most want to do right now?

- How can you bring your thoughts into actions?

Creative Minds

Oh yeah, more of my kind. We can seem scattered or introspective, messy or specifically organized. We may care deeply about one thing and care less about another. Yes, we can be random in our manner, but we have true meaning and an important purpose. Questing with us will require all 17 Strategies used as creatively as you can. I promise you will be invited on a magical journey with us at the lead!

My most important tip for you is to remember that real creative work requires honest and serious effort. Creative work is hard work and one has to have the passion to do it. So, flippant as we may appear, we're working diligently to sort out problems and face down challenges. It may look like fun (and we mostly think it is), but it is still difficult work to accomplish our artistic and lofty goals. We get stuck, depressed, lost, impoverished, confused, and disappointed. We may want to give up, or actually do so. We need encouragement to keep working because we are creative. It is not something we choose to be. And we bring meaning and purpose to life for all through our creative work. We identify and solve problems.

- What are you creating right now?
- What do you want to create in the next six months, year, decade?
- What have you discovered along your creative path?
- How do you define your creative purpose?
- How will you handle creative freeze?
- Where do you find your best inspiration?
- What's your plan for managing creative anxiety?

- Where do you find your ideas?

- When do you create?

- Who will support you financially?

- What kinds of people support you personally?

- Where do you find relaxation?

- What entertains you?

- How do you define being a creative person?

- What does your creative process mean?

- Why do you think people need to be creative?

- How do you define art?

- How do you define creativity?

- What creative dilemmas' are you working to solve right now?

- How do you record your creative process, learning, and meanings?

Customer Service

Customer service folks usually have a script to follow. So could you. Figure out what you want and the powerful simple questions you'll need to ask to get it, and then fire away! All 17 Strategies used in various combinations will help you with this type of power quest.

- Who knows how to figure out my problem?
- Do you speak English (Greek, French, Spanish, etc.)?
- Who do I speak to about a ___ problem?
- What is that person's name, direct phone number, fax number, and email address?
- What is your email address?
- What is your fax number?
- What is your mailing address?
- What is your name and employee number?
- Can I call back and speak to you directly?
- Who is your supervisor? How do I contact her directly?
- Can I look that up myself online?
- How do I file a complaint?
- How do I get _____?
- Where can I find that in writing and get a printed copy?
- How will you follow up with my request? Specifically by phone, mail, email, fax, in person?
- When can I expect your follow-up?

Dancers

I think dancers are amazing creatures who can translate life into movement. They study all things still and resonating to figure out how they can emulate them. They understand the nature of things through their rhythms. Many schools of thought speak about the universe as a series of vibrations. Dancers intuit this as fact because it is their reality. While all 17 Strategies will be helpful, I think paying particular attention to adding sensory cues to your questions will make them particularly powerful when questing with a movement artist. Questing with dancers is literally a moving experience that can bring you a new and delightful perspective.

- How will your body withstand that kind of movement?

- How much practice time do you need to regularly perform?

- Where do you find your best inspiration?

- Where would you like to dance?

- How do you define dancing?

- What are you favorite physical movements?

- What props help you the most?

- How much time do you spend dancing in a day?

- How has your movement changed over time?

- What will you do to adjust to your body's aging?

- What's your favorite rhythm?

- How do you like to warm up your body?

- What type of music or sounds do you like to dance to?

- What energizes you?

- How might your dancing be like poetry?

- What meanings do you give to specific movements?

- What purpose can you define for dancing through life?

Digital Artists

This type of artist was once thought of as someone who cheated at making real art. However, the magnificent tools and technologies we have today do take a skilled artist to master, and I believe that a digital artist has come into the world of true art. Let's face it, we all benefit by using their craft every day. Just look at the screen on your smartphone or watch the television. Their work is everywhere. Most people will encounter a digital artist at some point, whether for business cards, website design, a power point presentation, app, or some other technical tool. The 17 Strategies will once again be useful in questing with this vast, diverse group of people.

- Where do you find your best inspiration?
- Can you provide me with a breakdown of how you will illustrate my information?
- Can you suggest another way to present my material?
- What is your favorite creative habit?
- How long can you sit and work on the computer?
- Can you teach me how to perform this (be specific) task?
- What is your plan to earn a living from your art?
- How do you maintain your creativity?
- Who is your mentor?
- How do you find support from other artists?
- When will you have the work completed?
- How much do you charge for (be specific) and can you give me a breakdown of your charges by task?

- Will I own the copyright? Will you provide me with documentation to prove this?

- How can I check to make sure the imagery we choose is copyright free?

- When can I see a mockup of the work I requested?

Doctors

Many people have mixed opinions of the relationship they have with their doctors. It is my opinion that thinking through the type of relationship desired will yield a better communication style overall. I personally like to be responsible for my healthcare, and that means I expect my doctors to work on my team as valued partners. I want my doctors' expertise, not their approval, sanction, or belief system. They are highly paid service providers, and I expect them to be professional, skilled, and respect my intentions for the way I want to live my life. Using the 17 Strategies, I approach the quest with them like a job interview, because I am also a professional, whose time and concerns are equally important.

- Will you work with me on my healthcare team?
- Will you teach me about this condition?
- Can I email you with more questions?
- Will your nurse be available to help me?
- Who do I contact for my results?
- Could we work from my list first?
- Would you acknowledge all my good self-work?
- Are there any other options?
- Could you recommend another doctor for a second opinion?
- Can you support me if I decide to go an alternative route?
- What will that treatment cost?
- Can you reduce your fee?

- When will I need a follow-up?

- What can I expect during and after treatment?

- How do you resolve conflict?

- If you don't know the answer to my questions, will you tell me and then look into finding the answers?

- How do you prefer to follow up with me?

- Is there a direct way I can speak with you and not an employee or yours?

- Can you recommend another plan for my best health outcome?

- Can you work with me to implement a realistic healthcare plan?

Elders

Speak in a crisp, clear voice and look elderly people in the eye. Smile as you speak and repeat as necessary, exactly as you spoke your request the first time, using the same tone and words. The older the person, the more you may need to slow your speech. In addition, remember that hearing lower voice tones tends to erode as we age, so if you speak in a low voice, speak a little louder. We'll all most likely end up in some variant of sensory decline as we age, so remember you're looking in a mirror. How will you want to be questioned?

- Would you like some help?
- Do you need help?
- What will make you more comfortable?
- Can I call someone to help you?
- Do you need to sit down?
- Do you need a glass of water?
- Do you need directions?
- What have you enjoyed learning?
- How many places have you explored in your life?
- What do you want to discover right now?
- What are your favorite memories?
- Do you have any regrets? What and why?
- What would you do differently if you could start over?
- What are you learning about living a good long life?

- What details really mattered to you?

- What do you enjoy doing now?

- What was your favorite activity when you were thirty?

- Do you have children or grandchildren? What is that like for you?

- What makes you smile, laugh, cry, happy?

- What did your childhood smell like?

- What was the most amazing thing you every saw?

- What does life mean to you?

- Why do you think you came to be?

Employees

We need them, they make our business successful. We do need to learn and implement the skills that help them to help us produce our work. All 17 Strategies come into play when we quest with employees.

My tips: Remember to be professional and respectful. You set the standards within which they will perform. The employer/employee relationship dynamic is very much like dealing with adult children. Watch your role boundaries, tone of voice, and facial gestures. It's also like talking with your boss - you can be friendly, but not necessarily end up bosom buddies.

- What do you think would help your productivity improve?
- What can I do to help you learn?
- What can I do to inspire you?
- What can I offer as an incentive?
- How can I make your work environment more appealing?
- What would make you more comfortable?
- What are your suggestions to improve productivity?
- How do you define your job?
- Where do you want to be in your career in two years, five years, or ten?
- What do you have a real passion to do?
- What do you enjoy in your free time that helps you on the job?

- What do you feel are your most useful skillsets?

- How can we fully utilize your skills?

- What makes you want to come to work in the morning?

- What would you like to leave behind at the end of the day?

- What will you take home and enjoy besides your paycheck at the end of the week?

Fiber Artists

I started making fiber art long before it had an actual category in the art world. The richness of handling fibers truly adds a texture to one's creativity that somehow relates to the soul. Many of my fellow artists are making wonderful fiber art, and they are interesting to quest with because they love the fibrous nature of things, including powerful questions. Fibers run long or short, like telegraph wires once did, and connect in various places. The variety is endlessly lush and full of fertile opportunities to explore. I think many of my 17 Strategies probably became clear from my work with fiber, and therefore I know they'll be helpful along a power quest with anyone like a fiber artist.

- How will you get your tactile fix daily?
- How much fiber do you need to stay inspired and balanced?
- Do you plan on selling your art?
- How much money do you want to make from your art?
- Where do you find your best inspiration?
- How do you define being a fiber artist?
- What fibers excite you the most?
- What would you like to learn about?
- Who would you like to study with?
- Where is your passion for fiber art going?
- What's next on your creative journey?
- What have you learned about life from working with fiber?

- How many ways can you explain the meaning of your work by relating it to the nature of fiber?

- How many analogies to life have you discovered from working with fiber? What are they?

- If you were a fiber, what kind would you be?

- What do you feel the main purpose of fiber to be?

Financial Advisors

Financial advisors are human beings, like the rest of us. I hear so many folks cringe at the thought of talking with their advisor, and I think it's because it also means looking at the state of their financial wellbeing. These are two very different things. One is about money, a tangible means of barter, and the other is about a relationship.

Having a relationship with your advisor is a wonderful thing. It can let you know how they think and hopefully give you some specific information about how they think about serving you. Getting to know their likes and habits can help you make the decisions about your money, for which you're relying on their expertise. If you share like values, the whole experience can be one of pleasure, rather than just the oft dreaded bottom line.

Getting to know my advisor has been most enjoyable. I discovered he is a writer in his off time and has crafted somewhere around a half dozen books. We share similar family values, which I know because we've talked about his family. I have an idea about some of the things about life he questions because we've shared some interesting discussions about them. Furthermore, you guessed it - all of this started with a quest.

We began looking at the state of my financial empire, such as it is, and then the questions began about what I wanted to do with my life. Wow, that was exciting, and I wanted to understand how I could achieve my dreams. My advisor added up the cost factor, and together we made a plan to pull it together. Money, as I discovered, is actually a fluid thing. The more I can help it flow specifically into my dreams, the happier I'm going to be. My advisor is a welcome member of my personal team! And yep, all 17 Strategies can help.

- What is your hobby?
- If this were your money, what would you do to make an extra $1,000 over the next year?
- Where do you find your best inspiration?
- Have other clients taken these steps?
- What books have you read lately?
- What do you like to do on your vacations?
- Explain how stocks are rated?
- How do you define being a financial advisor?
- How much money will I need, and how will I save it?

Friends

Life is impossible without our friends, and a true friend needs nurturing. They are part of the soul in us and our work. They pick us up when we fall and steady us when we falter. They are our most trusted mirror reflecting the whole truth about us. They love us because of our flaws. All my 17 Strategies have been tested through friendships over the years. Friendships have been my ultimate critic, advisor, cheerleader, mentor, and lover. I owe a debt to my friends because without them I wouldn't have written this book.

Power questing with a friend can be tough during times of truth telling or sheer pleasure when we're at ease and life is feeling good.

- What do you value most about our friendship?
- What can we do to have some fun together?
- Where would you like your life to be this time next year?
- What kind of travel would you take if you could go anywhere?
- How do you feel happiness daily?
- What makes you smile?
- What do you do on a stormy night?
- What do you get from engaging your hobby?
- How would you like to be remembered?
- How can I support you in your efforts?
- How do I support you now?
- What does being friends mean to you?

- What can I do?

General Service Providers

We encounter these folks every day. I wrote the 17 Strategies to help with the variety of people we must work with to get the things we most want in our lives. Remember, general service providers aren't just order takers or voices on the phone. They are real people, too. Don't forget to compliment them when you can or make verbal note of something special about them to make your exchange personable. Follow the Strategies and you'll achieve success power questing with them.

- How is the day going for you?
- How long is your shift?
- What will you do after your shift today?
- Why are you working here?
- What do you enjoy about working here?
- How did you get into this line of work?
- What other jobs have you had?
- Did you train to do this work?
- Is it always this busy?
- How long did you train to do this work?
- How does this job enhance your favorite passion?
- If you could be doing anything you wished, what would you do?

Graphic Artists

Graphic artists used to be differentiated from digital artists years ago. That was before most of their style of art was computerized. I still think of them as a bit different, because many people can learn the technical skills but not all of them have the artistic ability to create from scratch. However, my questions do have overlap since so much of their profession does, too. Refer back to the section for digital artists for more questions and use the 17 Strategies to guide you, as well.

- Where do you find your best inspiration?
- How do you define being a graphic artist?
- How will you market your skills?
- Do you have a portfolio of your work?
- Who have you designed for?
- How long does it take?
- Do you make digital backups?
- What is your favorite type of client?
- What is your usual method to maintain your creativity?
- How do you handle copyright issues?

Hairstylists, Technicians, and Specialists

Hairstylists, Technicians, and other Specialists have received specialized training for their trades. They are professionals and deserve to be treated like any other skilled providers. Through my years of receiving service from this industry, I've found all 17 Strategies to be of use when I power quest with them.

Tip: Never tell them to do whatever they think about your appearance! I have it on good authority from an educator in this industry that this is a "red flag" comment. You do have an opinion - especially of what you don't want! Be respectful of their skill, but don't set them, or yourself, up for disaster.

- Where do you find your best inspiration?
- Do your feet ever get tired?
- How do you define being a hair, skin, nail, or other care professional?
- How long did you train?
- What's your favorite task?
- How do you maintain your creativity?
- What ideas do you have for my hair type in terms of cut, color, and care?
- How do you deal with creative burnout?
- What do you do for fun?
- What's your passion?
- If you retire from this profession, what will you do?

- How can I maintain this haircut, type of hair dye, or manicure?
- How do you use your creativity at work?

Hearing Challenged or ADD

I find these two groups of people to have a similar need when questioned in that they both need exact, verbatim repetition. This is hard, but DO NOT rephrase your words with each repetition. You will swamp your listener. This also works for anyone replying to you with a definitive "What?"

And I would like to add that this technique is necessary for anyone multitasking in our modern, sound bite world.

The questions you ask for a power quest with these folks aren't much different from any others. You just need to find the method of communication that works. While I don't speak sign language, I do know that the deaf will usually take your words literally, so leave out all unnecessary details.

Asking "what's going on?" is a bit too broad of a question.

Try starting with more specific, simple yes/no breakdowns of your quest.

- Are you feeling well today?
- Can you go out for a walk?
- Is work getting better?
- Do you need help?
- Move on to more details when it seems appropriate.
- What one thing can I do to help you today?
- What three items would you like to talk about?
- How much time would you like to spend doing this?

- When is the best time for you to do this work?
- Who else would you like to involve at this time?

Stop when it seems to frustrate your listener. You can always find another time to try again.

Lawyers Questing to Clients

"Legalese" is a difficult language to understand, and asking great questions of clients will be beneficial to the situational outcome. Simple and direct methods of questioning, to help your client understand that this will be a process without any true guarantee, will help your case. Remember, clients are just people and they're angry, scared, and upset about something, for which they believe you have expertise. You actually have experience with the process of sorting out the legalities of their situation. Outlining the detailed parts of the legal process and offering to be of service through the way you pose questions will become a learning opportunity for your client.

All 17 Strategies will come into play at one time or another while you work with clients. Be clear, repeat, ask clients to repeat back what you say, and be patient, because they're learning from you and may, at this moment, be in some way traumatized.

- What do you expect from my services?
- What do you expect from me personally?
- Do you understand the process?
- Will you need any help assembling your information?
- What kind of help will you need assembling your information?
- How do you imagine this legal process will change your life?
- What do you want from this process?
- What are you willing to do?
- Can you talk about that with strangers?

- Will you be happy with that outcome?

- What will you except?

- Do you understand what I've explained?

- How will you best be able to communicate with me or my legal team?

Lawyers

If you've ever had to litigate, you know the term "legal-ese" has real meaning. It's a difficult language to speak, much less understand, and asking great questions will help you get to the point of what you most need. You will greatly benefit from using all 17 Strategies throughout a legal process.

- What's the process?
- What's the expected timeline?
- Who can I call with questions? What's their contact information?
- What specific help will you provide me?
- What is expected of me?
- How much will it cost?
- Will you give me a breakdown of the costs?
- Will I have another option if I don't like the outcome?
- Can I stop/end the proceedings anytime I want? Will there be consequences of doing so?
- Can I take a break from the proceedings anytime I want?
- When will you expect payment?
- What is your complaint process?
- What recourse will I have if I don't feel I'm getting appropriate service from you?
- If I want (a specific) outcome (be clear about this), will this legal action provide it?

Massage Therapists

Receiving a massage is a very personal thing. It's important to quest clearly and powerfully with your massage therapist about what you specifically want or don't want. This is the type of situation where miscommunication can cause an eruption of emotion. The full list of 17 Strategies can be useful to negotiate in a powerful way.

- What can I expect from your service before, during, and after?

- Will my privacy be respected?

- Will you explain the difference between the various massages you offer?

- How will we communicate about the type or intensity of touch I want during the massage?

- Where do you find your best inspiration?

- How do you define being a massage therapist?

- How long did you train to do this type of work?

- What other training do you want to do?

- What do you like most about what you do?

- What do you look for in an ideal client?

- What parts about your work are humorous?

- Can you teach me about what I can do to take care of my body (be specific)?

Managers

Just like employers, bosses, and parents, managers are in that gray zone of relationships angled somewhere between authority and friend. The 17 Strategies, along with referencing the specific types of quests mentioned above in this book, will provide you with plenty of helpful resources to powerfully quest. If you are a manager, or if you need to speak to your manager, these power questions can be tailored to your circumstance and guide you.

- What is your objective?
- What do you value about me as a team member?
- What role shall I take in this project?
- What is our projected timeline?
- What interdependencies do I need to be aware of?
- When do you want me to report?
- Who do you want me to report to?
- What else do I need to know?
- Why did you choose me for this job?
- Where will I find the resources that you want me to use for this project?
- What are the specific deadlines I need to know?

Men

Ladies, don't raise your voice and don't speak in a high-pitched, squeaky toned voice. It is painful to men - akin to a dog whistle to a dog's ears. Use as few words as possible. Their brains will tune out too many sounds, and they simply won't hear your requests. Men aren't stupid; they just work differently from you, so respect their diverseness. Learn to get to the point and leave out the emotion. For men, hearing the details will come much later in your quest to share information.

Tips: Men like yes/no questions best. Be satisfied that this is the answer—for now. Watch out for your internal judge as you speak, because men will see your criticism on your face, and they will shut down—who wouldn't? Wear a pleasant poker face when you talk to them.

Note: I wrote sections for men and women with some specific and simplified information that both sexes can use to better communicate with one another. I recommend that both read each other's section to gain a better understanding of how to power question the other.

The best question asked of a man:

"Would you like me to ask someone else?" This works because there is no assumption or predetermined judgment about his ability.

The best question that a man asked:

"Can I help you with that?" I love this question because the man asking isn't trying to takeover and fix it, but rather be helpful to the cause.

- Would you do ___ by ___?
- Would you listen to me talk about ___ for 10 Minutes?

- Can you help me ___? (Be specific about what you want in a few words.)

- Do you want to talk right now?

- Would you like me to be quiet right now?

- When would be a good time to ___? (Be specific about what you want in a few words.)

- Could you please take out the trash tonight before ten o'clock?

- Can you pick up dinner from ____ on your way home?

Mentor

Good mentors are like muses. They guide us and inspire us to do our greatest work. They can see our potential before we can. If you're lucky enough to have a good one, milk them for all they're worth. And revel in the joy they help you bring to the world. The 17 Strategies can help you navigate your power quests with them, and you might learn a few more great questions from them. Celebrate them and most of all work hard with them. Show them your gratitude often.

- How do you see us working together?
- How did you accomplish all of ___? (Be specific.)
- What are your most important habits?
- How do you define your role with me?
- What are some of your biggest challenges?
- What did you have to learn to meet success?
- How do you see us working together?
- How do you define yourself as my mentor?
- What do you want to get from this experience?
- What can I expect from you during this experience?
- What would you like me to do to make this a successful process for you?
- What am I missing?
- How does this process work best for you?
- What's your preferred method of me contacting you?

Musicians

Musical personalities are very much like dancers, except that they interpret the universal rhythms into sound. Accountants, engineers, and surgeons also may operate this way. They approach life in a mathematical or sequential manner and power questioning them in this way will be beneficial to your outcome. All 17 Strategies can be helpful questing with them, and using your creativity and playfulness will be most enjoyable. Refer to sections for dancers, and other artists for more powerful questions.

- How much daily practice time do you need?

- Where do you find your best inspiration?

- Do you have the support you need to make your music?

- What is your favorite melody?

- How many instruments do you play?

- What instrument would you like to learn?

- Will you sell your musical services?

- What do you play for your own pleasure?

- How do you define being a musician?

- What natural sounds help you create your music?

- If you were a sound, what sound would you be?

Painters

The soul of what I am is a painter. I may have as much paint in my veins as I usually wear. I like paint because it changes the surface enough to reflect back something different. In many ways, it is like a great and powerful question. All of my 17 Strategies have been crafted through my own experience of creative work. You can utilize interchangeably most of the questions you'll find in other artisan sections for any other type of artist, creative person, or visionary.

- What work do you want to complete?
- When do you paint best?
- Do you have a plan to paint?
- How long is it healthy for you to paint?
- What elements help you paint your best?
- Will you sell your work?
- Do you have a strategy to sell your work?
- How long do you need to complete your painting?
- How can you insure your timeline is realistic?
- How can you make your studio space workable?
- Where do you get your inspiration?
- What will maintain you while you work on your painting?
- How does your creative schedule fit in with the rest of your day?
- How does making your art mesh with your regular job?
- What will give you balance?

- How does it feel when you sell your work?
- How much do you need to sell to pay your bills?
- How do you define being a painter?
- What is the purpose of your art?
- Why do you paint?
- What do you like most about painting?
- What do you find least appealing about your creative work?
- What is your creative process?
- How do you define creative purpose?
- What is your favorite painting?
- What do you want your creative legacy to be?

Patients

Most of us have, or will be, a person in need of the care of skilled professionals in order to get well. Navigating this terrain in our lives can be especially difficult because we are not at our best when ill. As I explained earlier in this book, I had a head injury that led me to discover the 17 Strategies, so I understand how a patient might need to use them to powerfully quest her way back to health. The following power questions are designed to be asked of a patient, but can also be restated to be asked by the patient to her care provider.

- What do you hope to make different in your life after we try this treatment?
- What do you hope to get from these visits?
- What do you expect you'll gain from these tests?
- How can I explain this to you in order to make it easy for you to understand?
- What does feeling well look like to you?
- Would you like me to write this down for you?
- What small healthy steps have you taken this week?
- Where do you want to be next year?
- How can I help you to continue to reach your goals?
- What kind of support do you need?
- Would you like my help?
- What works for you?
- What is a realistic self-care plan for you during the next week?

Physical Trainers

Physical trainer is an interesting profession that has come about during the past few years. I think it profoundly says something about our cultural shift toward bettering our individuality. All of the 17 Strategies can be useful for different types of training situations. Since trainers are also service providers, you can interchange and use any of the questions posed in the other service oriented sections.

- What attracts you to this job?
- What inspiration do you take from this career?
- What is your ideal process?
- Will you have patience with me?
- What inspiration will you give me?
- Will you give me honest feedback?
- How do you define your ideal client?
- How do you define being a physical trainer?
- What's the average length of time we'll work together?
- What do you expect of me?
- What can I expect from you during the process?
- How can I contact you outside our meetings?

Quilters

These lovely people endeavor to wrap the world in beautiful comfort by cutting bits of fabric and then lovingly piecing them into cozy warmth. Quilters are true artisans, and all 17 Strategies work for you to communicate with them, as well as the lists of power questions for other artists.

- Where do you find your best inspiration?
- How do you define being a quilter?
- How much fabric is enough?
- Do you like working within a group of quilters?
- What's your favorite quilt pattern?
- What's your favorite quilting technique?
- Who do you like quilting for?
- What is your favorite project?
- What part of the process do you like best?
- What brings you the most joy from your quilting?
- What's your most useful quilting tool?
- How would you define the true value of your quilts?

Sculptors

Sculptors are special artists. I've always loved creating with this media, but could never figure out how I could stay with it due to its space and cost issues. I admire those who have, and I find their ability to see from all perspectives to create in three dimensions amazingly refreshing. Like the other previously mentioned artists, most certainly, any and all of the 17 Strategies can help you power quest with sculptors, and they will bring you to new valleys of discovery through the quest process.

- What will inspire you?
- How long will it take to complete your project?
- How will you fund it?
- What will help you manage your creative balance during the time frame between start and finish?
- How will you make a living from your art?
- Who will help you?
- How do you define being a sculptor?
- How will you keep physically fit to do your work?
- What do you see when you look at a pile of stone, clay, or wood?
- What is a fitting legacy for a sculptor?

Store Clerks

"The key to success is to get out into the store and listen to what the associates have to say. It's terribly important for everyone to get involved. Our best ideas come from clerks and stock boys." — Sam Walton

Store clerks can cause a change in your shopping experience. Sure, they have a job to do, but they also have a story to tell and, if you question them powerfully, you might enjoy listening to it as you get what you want answered. The 17 Strategies definitely help power quests with store clerks.

- How is your day going?
- Could you please show me where ___ is?
- Do you work on a commission?
- Do you have a business card?
- How long is you shift?
- Is this the job you trained for?
- How long have you worked here?
- How do you remember all those codes?
- How can I put in a good word for you?
- Is this the item on sale?
- Can I return this within 30 days?
- What is the return policy?
- Do you like working here?

Students

Teachers serve students, and students make the success of the teacher. The relationship can be as stilted as any of the previously mentioned authority situations. At one time or another, all of the 17 Strategies will come up while navigating teacher/student relationships. The list of power questions below are designed to ask a student, but could easily be redirected to a teacher.

- How are you managing the workload I assigned? (Note this is different from asking "How is it going?")

- What could I do different to make this information more applicable to your life?

- How do you want to take in this information so you are best able to apply it in your life?

- What do you think is the most interesting aspect of this lesson?

- How could you present this material differently?

- What else would you like to learn about this topic?

- What does this lesson inspire you to do?

- How will you use this material in your life?

- Can you think of someone in your life, now or in the future, who could benefit from your knowing this information?

- How do you suppose this information will change the future?

- In what ways do you think this information will be changed in the future?

- What would make your learning experience more valuable?

Teachers

I looked for, and was fortunate to find, a special type of degree that was self-designed. This means that, as a student, I planned and designed my own specific curriculum, according to the college guidelines. Of course, I had many advisors who worked closely with me to develop the studies I would need to accomplish. The beauty of this educational style is that it required me to ask very powerful and specific questions to accomplish my degree program. A significant requirement of my program was to question my teachers and interview them before we worked together. This opportunity was an important part of my education, and I encourage students to find ways they can incorporate asking power questions of their educators. After all, education is a business contract that benefits from good communication and exploration.

These power questions are set up for students to ask of their instructors, and, just like in the previous section, they use the full 17 Strategies. Many questions students ask teachers are interchangeable for teachers to use with students.

- Where could I look for more information?
- How can I get in touch with you?
- How do you prefer me to contact you?
- What references do you recommend?
- When is the work due?
- How do you grade?
- Do you have other students' samples that I could look at?
- Will you be recording your lectures?

- Do I need to attend every class?

Teenagers

These creatures are special cases, because many of their human parts realign while you watch. Teenagers are very fragile in spite of many characteristics that would say they're rough and tumble. Their minds are a slush pile of emotional thoughts. Have some empathy when you question them, and ease into a conversation with simple questions. Once they follow your lead, you can move up to the more complex requests that require additional thought from them.

- Would you like to grab a hamburger?

Give them a simple choice next.

- Joe's or Shelly's?

Once the meal is well underway, you can ask more engaging thoughtful answers.

- What do you like best about Joe's burgers?

It's also important to recognize that while they don't truly have a clue where they will be next year, much less in an hour, they do have opinions. In fact, they never seem short on their own views. For them, it's all about trying out the sensation of their next thought, and your response is very much a part of the experiment. So think through your questing with them so that you can get the outcome you most need, rather than what you want.

- What do you think is the best time to leave for school?
- What's the best time for you to wake up on Saturday?

The brain of a teenager is a highly specialized microscope dwelling on the literal thought under the slide. Anything you ask that has an implication will be met with a barrage of smug wit. This is only their defense, because they can't take in all the complexities of implied quests when they have every little syllable picked apart. If you ask questions that require them to share what they're thinking right now, you will get what you need and allow them to illustrate for themselves that they need to find their own answers. As a mother, I found out that this type of modeling was helpful for my kids, and it lessened the stress I felt as a parent when I needed information to help the family run smoothly.

Once you have a flow going, you can develop the power question shortcuts most adults seem to gravitate toward. These are best saved for the end of a conversation.

- What would you like to do?
- What time would you like to leave?
- When would you like to get up?
- What sounds like fun to you?

Terminally Ill

The terminally ill and their caregivers are very similar. Both are helplessly facing a death of what was, and looking into a future of unknowns thrust upon them. They are no longer in control of their lives, but in a position of reacting to life as it comes at them. I feel many of my 17 Strategies relate to this situation, because oddly, I felt the person I was before my head injury died, and I was becoming someone new. Questions in the caregiver section will complement questions for this group, as well.

- What would you like to talk about?

- How are you doing with your situation?

- What do you, or your family, need right now?

- What's the hardest thing for you?

- What would make you more comfortable?

- What additional support do you or your family need?

- How can I be there for you and your family?

- Would you like me to share what's been going on in my life?

- What do you miss about life before the illness?

- Is there anything you'd like me to remember about you?

- Can I share with you what I'll always hold in my heart about you?

Weavers

These artisans have more of a mathematical approach to their creativity. Weavers can follow a long thread from beginning to end and make it all come together by jumping aside for patterns to emerge and hopping over and under for strength and cohesion to form. Their way of thinking is quite fascinating. Many of the 17 Strategies will help you power quest with them, just like they help quest with bankers or other linear thinkers.

- What will you do with all your thrums?

- Where do you find your best inspiration?

- How does the rhythm of your weaving align with the rhythm of your life?

- How do you define being a weaver?

- If the warp and weft were your favorite people, who would they be?

- What are your favorite techniques?

- How does weaving illustrate your life?

- Where will you sell your weaving?

- What do you like about weaving?

- How would you describe the people who value your work?

Women

Guy's, don't raise your voice and please pay attention to your facial expression. So many men look angry or in pain when women speak. This unhappy face will affect women in ways unpleasant for both of you. Their thinking brains will turn off, and they'll simply react - emotionally! They won't hear your requests. Learn to put on a happy, relaxed face, and you'll get better responses from women.

In addition, remember women are not stupid, they just work differently from you, so respect their diverse richness. They get the whole enormous landscape at the precise moment you're talking to them — not just your specialized piece. They are wired for multitasking thought, so it's important you keep pace with them. If you stall or rush them, they'll get flooded with feelings.

Tips:

Relax and smile when a woman is talking to you. You'll both like the feeling.

Remember that women are powerfully capable of creation. Hold respect for them and what you can make happen together.

These are the best questions a man can ask a woman.

- How are you feeling today?
- What would you like me to do about that?
- Shall I just listen or take action?

Writers

Well, I guess I fit this category of artists, too. Power questing with writers is quite the magical trip. Writers ask powerful questions in order to write, and then they write out all the possible answers, sorting out the verbal trinkets into treasures. All 17 Strategies can come into play when you power quest with a writer, which by now you've fully experienced through reading my book.

- What will you do with writers block?
- Where do you find your best inspiration?
- What is your normal writing practice?
- What are your favorite writing prompts?
- What can you do with your old stories?
- What tools or props help you write?
- When will you know your work is finished?
- Who is your main audience?
- Who do you want to please the most with your work?
- How will you make money selling your work?
- How many pieces do you write at any given time?
- How do you define being a writer?
- How does your story end?

About the Author

Sandy Nelson is an Artist, Creativity and Life Purpose Coach, Speaker, and Inspirational Writer. She maintains a coaching practice in the Minneapolis area and around the world, as well as leads Creativity workshops and Self-Empowerment retreats. Her course *Becoming Resilient,* offered through DailyOm, is the culmination of more than 20 years of experience. Sandy has been interviewed on BlogTalkRadio, and she regularly blogs on creativity for JenningsWire and her own blog Meet Your Muse. She also created and teaches at The Play Wizardly School, where you can find her *Permission to Play Now* courses and *Get to the Point Chats with Coach Sandy* audio series, and she produces her own quarterly newsletter The Muse News.

Author's Note

Thank you for reading my book. I hope you've enjoyed learning about how you can *Ask Power Questions,* and that you've gathered a few good nuggets to help you on your life journey toward success. Won't you please take a moment to leave me a review at your favorite retailer?

Choose your favorite way to connect with me:

I would love to hear from you about your thoughts and experiences, as well as to answer your questions, on this topic of how to ask powerful questions. Please, feel free to contact me directly.

Email me at: sandy@meetyourmuse.com.

Visit my web site and sign up for the Muse News Newsletter: www.meetyourmuse.com

Subscribe to my blog:
http://sandysmymblog.wordpress.com

Link with me at LinkedIn:
www.linkedin.com/in/SandyNelsonMuse

Tweet me on Twitter: https://twitter.com/thePlayWizard

Google with me at Google+:
https://google.com/+SandyNelson

Friend me on Facebook:
www.facebook.com/sandy.nelson.90260

Enjoy visual inspiration with me on Pinterest:
https://pinterest.com/meetyourmus0328

www.ingramcontent.com/pod-product-compliance
Lightning Source LLC
Chambersburg PA
CBHW070504200326
41519CB00013B/2716